The Norv

[

Thomas Peck

Alpha Editions

This edition published in 2022

ISBN: 9789356906143

Design and Setting By

Alpha Editions

www.alphaedis.com

Email - info@alphaedis.com

Contents

DEDICATION

To Jeremiah Ives, jun. Esq.

SIR,

The High Office of Mayor of this City, so honourably filled by yourself, claims the respectful acknowledgement of the Publisher of this work, who is happy to receive permission of dedicating to you this publication; and is, with all due respect,

Your very Obliged
and Obedient Servant,
THOMAS PECK.

INTRODUCTION

The difficulty of finding the precise Address of the Inhabitants of so populous a city as Norwich, the general utility of a Directory, and the spirit of Public Improvement which has of late appeared, have, at the present period, rendered this publication peculiarly necessary.

The contents are fully expressed in the title-page, the arrangement is adapted to every capacity, and will be found to answer every useful purpose.

The houses in each street are all regularly numbered, beginning on the right hand, and returning on the left, with a few exceptions for the sake of convenience.

The boards, with the names of the streets, lanes, and thorough-fares, which are now correctly painting, will be put up at the corner, or entrance of each; and the whole will be completed as soon as possible.

It is with the greatest pleasure we review the many alterations for public convenience which have been recently made: in particular—

The Reservoir in Chapel-field, which, by the aid of a steam-engine, is always filled, and supplies the highest parts of the city with water.

The taking down of Brazen-doors, St. Stephen's, St. Giles', St. Benedict's, St. Augustine's, Pockthorpe, Bishop, and King-street Gates; thereby admitting a current of salubrious air; and if such parts of the wall round as are not built against were to be removed, it would be still more complete.

The Paving of the Gentlemen's Walk with Scotch granate.

The taking down of the cumbrous Weigh-house in the Hay-market, which ought now to bear another title, and erecting a house for the purpose on the Castle-Dykes, with an elegant engine, which acts with a steel-yard under ground, and the carriage placed on the level above.

The widening of the street, now Orford-street, leading from Hog-hill to the Castle-dykes.

The opening from off the Castle-meadow into King-street.

The levelling of the old houses at the back of Messrs. Gurney's, at the foot of the Castle hill.

The new Flour Mill, worked by steam, which is erected, by subscription, near Black Friar's Bridge, for better supplying the city with flour.

And the new Horse Barracks, without Pockthorpe.

Not to mention the superior appearance which the Shops in the Market-place, London-lane, and other parts of the city, now assume.

We have authority to say, that, the two Old Workhouses being in a ruinous state, it is the intention of the Court of Guardians to apply to Parliament for an Act to enable them to build One New and Complete Workhouse—the spot fixed on is the Gilden-croft.

Much has been done under the gloomy aspect of War; but from the establishment of Peace, we ardently hope to see our native Commerce revived, every necessary improvement carried into effect, and the splendour of our ancient city equal to its opulence.

We here present our Readers with a Retrospect of the PROPOSED *Public Improvements.*

On the 23d of January, 1800, John Herring, Esq. then Mayor, summoned a General Meeting of the Inhabitants, at the Guildhall, to consider of the propriety of applying to Parliament for an Act for the better paving, cleaning, lighting, and watching of the city; for removing and preventing annoyances and obstructions, and for regulating hackney coaches.

At this meeting, a committee of twenty-one gentlemen was appointed to consider of the plan proposed by the Mayor, and to make a report, to a future general meeting, of the result of its opinion.

This committee had several meetings, in which it very minutely investigated the subject submitted to its consideration: it employed proper persons to estimate the expence of paving a particular district, and stationed men at fourteen entrances into the city, to ascertain the actual number of carriages, horses, &c. of every description, which passed and repassed during a week, that a fair calculation might be made of the expence to be incurred, and of the funds to meet it.

The result of the labours of this committee was laid before a general meeting of Inhabitants, on the 3d of March following, in a report, which stated the expediency of applying for an Act for the following purposes:

I. To empower a Deputy Mayor to be appointed in certain cases.

II. To empower the Mayor, or the Deputy Mayor, with one Justice, to adjourn the Sessions in the absence of the Recorder and Steward.

III. To better regulate the watch.

IV. To better light the city.

V. To better regulate the sweeping and cleansing of the city.

		£
The present expence		
of lighting		632
of watching		550
of sweeping		700
		1882
The future expence, under the new regulations proposed by the committee,		
Lighting	840	
Watching	730	1770
Sweeping	200	
would amount to a saving of		112

And on a supposition that scavengers would undertake the sweeping, &c. for the produce of the muck, the saving would be £312.

VI. To new pave the city.

The expence of the new pavement, with foot paths on each side of the streets, the middle of the streets crowning, and the removing of all obstructions, was estimated at £55,000, on an actual survey and valuation, made by Messrs. Stannard and Athow; and this estimate was, in the opinion of Mr. Hamerton, an eminent Paviour in London, very fair and correct.

To defray such an apparent heavy expence, the committee, proposed levying a toll on carriages, horses, &c. coming to and going from the city, in the following proportions:

	d.
One horse	0½
Cart with one horse	1
Cart with three or more horses	1½
A one-horse chaise or gig	1½
A waggon	2

A four-wheel carriage	2
A score beasts, &c.	2

The annual produce of these tolls, deducing the expence of Houses, Collectors, &c. was estimated at £1715.

The committee likewise proposed a rate, not exceeding 6d. in the pound, per quarter, on the landlords and occupiers of houses, &c. within the city (exclusive of the hamlets), the annual produce of which was calculated at £3000; so that the whole expence, under the proposed bill, would have stood thus:

	£	£
For lighting, watching, and cleansing	1770	
For keeping in repair such parts of the city as could not be immediately paved	1000	2770
Produce of tolls	1715	
of rate	3000	4715

Leaving for the immediate commencement of paving, the sum of £1945; which sum would have been increased by the annual payment of a certain sum by the Corporation, the Bishop, and Dean and Chapter, for such parts of the city now repaired by them; and by the annual decrease of the sum of £1000, in proportion as the new pavement was completed.

The committee concluded this well-digested report by stating its opinion, that no time should be lost in applying to Parliament; but as it had several other matters under consideration, it begged leave to be permitted to make a final report at some future time.

The general meeting concurred, after some deliberation, with the committee; and a petition was signed by most of the Inhabitants of the city, for leave to bring in a bill for the several purposes mentioned in the report.

Unfortunately, however, the petition could not, from some unforeseen circumstances, be presented that sessions; it being a standing order of the House of Commons, that no such bill could be brought before Parliament, unless notice of it had been given at the preceding Michaelmas sessions: but it was suggested, seemingly from authority, that such notice, in the present instance, might be dispensed with, provided the city would abandon the toll, or a tonnage on goods.

To such a restriction, the committee would not submit; it therefore resolved to postpone the petition to the next sessions of Parliament, and, in the mean time, that a committee of Country Gentlemen, to be appointed at the ensuing sessions, should be requested to meet a sub-committee of the city, to hold a conference on the subject.

This conference took place, and after a number of queries had been proposed by the Country Gentlemen, to all of which satisfactory answers were returned in writing; notice of the intended application to Parliament was ordered to be affixed on the doors of the Sessions Hall, both in the county and city.

The committee however soon found, notwithstanding it had given what if deemed the most satisfactory answers to the queries suggested by the Country Gentlemen, that the bill would meet with the most determined opposition from the county; nor did it appear that the opposition could be obviated, unless the whole expence to be incurred by any intended improvements was confined to the city only. With such an opposition, the committee had no hopes of success; and whatever sentiments it might entertain of the liberality of the Country Gentlemen, who would, with the county at large, have materially partaken of the benefits and advantages attending the improvements, though they were unwilling to bear the most trifling part of the expence of them, it did not choose to hazard the experiment of a contest.

The committee, however, had the object entrusted to it too much at heart to abandon it entirely: it therefore relinquished all the former part of the proposed regulations, and confined itself solely to what it deemed the most expedient—the New Pavement. The Committee submitted a report on that subject only to a general meeting, on the 15th of December, 1800, the substance of which was, that, to carry the plan proposed into execution, a rate not exceeding 3d. in the pound, per quarter, on the rack-rent, should be levied on the Inhabitants of the city, at such times only when the poor rate was within 6s. per pound, per quarter, for three successive quarters.

At length, from considerations of the distress of the times, this truly interesting business was deferred, but we have authority, and are happy to say, that it will be resumed in a more favourable season.

We cannot quit this subject without observing, that the arduous and unremitted assiduity of the Gentlemen forming the Committee, met the warmest approbation of their fellow citizens, and afforded a prospect that, at a future period, their labours for so desirable an object would ultimately be accomplished.

References to the Churches in the Plan. [0]

A	St. Martin's at Oak	S	St. Peter's Hungate
B	St. Augustine's	T	St. Michaels at Plea
C	St. Mary's	U	St. George's Tombland
D	St. George's Colegate	V	St. Simon and Jude's
E	St. Saviour's	W	St. Martin's by Palace
F	St. Paul's	X	St. Helen's
G	St. James'	Y	St. Giles'
H	St. Edmund's	Z	St. Peter's Mancroft
I	St. Clement's	I.	St. Stephen's
K	St. Michael's Coslany	II.	St. John's Timberhill
L	St. Swithin's	III.	All Saints'
M	St. Margaret's	IV.	St Michael's at Thorn
N	St. Lawrence'	V.	St. John's Sepulchre
O	St. Benedict's	VI.	St. Peter's Southgate
P	St. Gregory's	VII.	St. Etheldred's
Q	St. John's Maddermarket	VIII.	St. Julian's
R	St. Andrew's	IX.	St. Peter's per Mountergate

Public Buildings and Offices.

French church	Quakers' meeting
Dutch church	Guildhall
Grammar school	Fish-market
Methodist meeting	Stamp office
Deanery	Bethel
Excise office	Theatre-Royal
St. Giles' hospital	Assembly house
Boys' hospital	Castle, county gaol, and shire-house
Girls' hospital	Norfolk and Norwich hospital
Doughty's hospital	Private lunatic house
Court of Request office	Bridewell
Presbyterian new meeting	Post office
Independent meeting	St. Andrew's work-house
Anabaptist meeting	Roman Catholic chapel
Duke's Palace work-house	St. John's work-house
City gaol	

Alphabetical List of the Streets, Lanes, &c. in the City of Norwich.

All Saints' Green	Fye-bridge-street	Peacock-street
Almhouse lane	Fye-bridge-quay	Pigg-street
Andrew's St. Bridge-str.	George's St. Bridge-str.	Pitt-lane
— Chancel-str.	George's St. Ch. alley	Pottergate-street
— Plain	Gildencroft	Privy-lane
— Steps	Gildencroft-lane	Pudding-lane
Anne's lane	Gildengate-street	Queen-street
— steps	Giles' St. Hill	Rampant Horse Back str.
Augustine's St. Ch. row	Giles' St. street	Rampant Horse street
— street	Giles' St. Back-street	Red-Lion-lane
Back of the Inns	Giles' St. Broad-street	Red-Well-street
Bank-place	Giles' St. road	Rising-Sun-lane
Barrack-street	Goat lane Upper	Rose lane
Ber-street	Goat lane Lower	Rosemary-lane
Bethel-street	Golden-Ball-lane	St. Saviour's lane
Bishopgate-street	Golden-Dog lane	St. Saviour's Church lane
Botolph-street	Green's lane	St. Saviour's Ch. alley
Bracondale	Gregory's St. Ch. alley	Scole's Green
Bridewell-alley	Griffin-lane	Shuttle lane
Briggs' lane	Gun-lane	Snailgate-street
Buff-coat-lane	Hall's End	Southgate-street

Bull-lane	Haymarket	St. Stephen's street
Butcher's market	Heigham-street	St. Stephen's Back-street
Castle-dykes	Hog hill	St. Stephen's Ch. alley
Castle meadow	Horn's lane	St Stephen's road
Chapel-field	Hungate-street	Stepping-lane
Chapel-field-lane	John's St. Timberhill	Surry street
Chapel street	Jail hill	Surry-street mewse
Charing-cross	Jenkin's lane	Surry-street Upper
Cherry-lane	King-street	Swan-lane
Clement's St. Ch. alley	Lady's lane	St. Swithin's lane
Close Upper	Lady's row	St. Swithin's Church lane
Close Lower	Lawrence St. Ch. alley	St. Swithin's Church alley
Cockey-lane	Lawrence St. lane	Theatre-square
Cockey-lane Little	Life's Green	Timberhill street
Cockril lane	London lane	Tombland
Colegate-street	Maddermarket street	Tooley-street
Common Pump	Magdalen-street	Upper market
Common Pump-street	Margaret's St. lane	Upper market-street
Common Staithe Old	Margaret's St. Ch. alley	Wastlegate-street
Common Staithe New	Mariner's lane	Water-lane, St George's
Cook's lane	Market-lane	Water-lane, St James'
Coslany-street	Market place	Water-lane, King-street
Coslany Bridge-street	Martin's St. street	Water-lane, St Martin's
Cow-hill	Martin's St. lane	Weaver's lane

Cowgate-street	Martin's St. by Pal. plain	Westwick street Lower
Cross lane	Martin's St. by Pal. str.	Westwick street Upper
Dove-lane	Mary's St. Plain	Westwick Back-street
Duke's Palace	Mary's St. Church alley	Wherry-staithe
Elmhill-street	Mich St. Cos. Ch. alley	White Friars' Bridge st.
Elmhill-lane	Michael's St. Thorn lane	White-Lion-lane
Faith's St. lane	Music-House-staithe	Wilkes's lane
Field-square	Muspole-street	Willow-lane
Finket-street	Nailor's lane	World's End lane
Fish-market	New-Mills'-lane	Wymer-street
Fisher's lane	Orford-street	
Fishgate-street		

THE NORWICH DIRECTORY.

ABBS Z. Boot and Shoe Maker, No. 72, Coslany-Street

Abel Anthony, Cabinet-Maker, 5, Upper Westwick street

Abram John, Patten-maker, 27, Magdalen-street

Adair William, Esq. Trowse Newton and Caldecot Bucks

Adams and Bacon, Coach makers, 3, St. Stephen's road

Adcock and Gapp, Dyers, 7, Coslany-Bridge-street

Adcock James, Royal-Oak, 27, St. Augustine's road

Adcock William, Hair-dresser, 60, St. Giles'

Addey John, Linen-Draper, 4, London-lane

Adlam John, Gardner, 18, St. Augustine's street

Aggs John Gurney, Iron-Foundery, St. Faith's lane

Aggs Thomas, Linen-Manufacturer, 10, Pitt-street

Alden Thomas, Butcher, 9, Fish-Market

Alderson James, M.D. 3, Snailgate-street

Alderson Mrs. 11, Gildengate-street

Alderson John, Plumber, &c. 20, Upper-Market

Alderson J. K. Plumber, &c. 6, Hog-hill

Alderson William, Mounter, 18, ditto

Aldhouse Stephen, Surgeon, &c. 2, Wymer-street

Aldhouse Stephen, 92, Upper Heigham

Aldhouse Stephen, at the Lamb. 51, Coslany-street

Aldis John, Baker, 7, St. Margaret's Church

Aldred James, Hemp-cloth Manufacturer, Shuttle-lane, and in Weaver's lane on Saturdays

Aldrich John, Whitesmith, 15, Dove-lane

Alexander Stephen, Shoemaker, St. Stephen's road

Allman Samuel, Baker, 67, Coslany-street

Allen Richard, Tailor and Draper, 21, London-lane

Allen Charles, Esq. 4, Upper Surry-street

Allen Robert, Tailor, &c. 36, Pottergate-street

Allen William, Boot and Shoe maker, 48, St. Stephen street

Allum John, Tea-Dealer and Confectioner, 57, Bethel-street

Allwood Thomas, Shopkeeper, 22, Lower Close

Ames Daniel, 19, St. Martin's Plain

Amyott Thomas, Attorney, 13, Upper Close

Amy Thomas, Cooper, 99, Magdalen-street

Anderson John Fullick, at the Norwich Volunteer, 29, All Saint's Green

Andrews William, 44, St. Stephen's street

Angel John and Son, Curriers, 5, Golden Ball-lane

Angell Joseph, King's Head, 12, Gildengate-street

Angier James, Merchant, Dwelling-House, 42, Snailgate-str.

Anguish Rev. 12, Upper Close

Annis John, Bookseller, 5, London-lane

Ansell John, Plumber, &c. 12, Dove-lane

Appleton John, Hatter, &c. 5, Back of the Inns

Arnold William, 10 and 11, St. Stephen's road

Artis John, Boot and Shoe maker, 24, Rampant-Horse-street

Athow John, jun. Stone and Marble Mason, 12, Back of the Inns

Atkins William, Shawl Manufacturer, 28, Lower Westwick-street

Atkinson John, Attorney, 191, King-street

Aves Jeremiah, Trumpet Inn, 40, St. Stephen's street

Ayton William, Coppersmith, Brazier, and Tin-plate Worker, 4, Briggs' lane

B

Back Thomas and Co. Grocers, Tea-Dealers, and Tallow-Chandlers, 3 and 4, Hay-market

Back James, Importer of Foreign Wines and Spirits, 3, Hog-hill

Back William, Surgeon, Wilkes's lane, near Bank-place

Back Mrs. 4, Bowling-green house, Chapel-field house

Bacon Richard, Auctioneer, Appraiser, Printer, Bookseller, Binder, and Stationer, 12, Cockey-lane

Bacon Leonard, Wine-Merchant, 30, St. Giles's Wine Vaults, in Chapel-field

Bacon Thomas, Ginger-bread Baker, 4, St. Stephen's street

Bailey William, Shawl and Bombazine Manufacturer, 5, White-Lion-lane

Baker Henry, Gold and Silver smith, 15, Market-place

Baker Benjamin, Gardner and Seedsman, 5, Queen-street

Baldy Edmund, Dyer, 62, Gildengate-street

Baletti Anthony, Frame-maker, 13, Pottergate-street

Balls Thomas, House-Broker, 7, St. Martin's by Palace

Balls James, Tailor, 2, Snail-gate-street

Banham James, Pump-maker, 146, King-street

Banton John, at the Crown, 29, St. George's Bridge street

Barber Thomas, Attorney, 2, St. Stephen's Back-street

Barber George, Silversmith, 3, London-lane

Bardwell Edward, Boot and Shoe maker, 13, Lower Close

Barker Mrs. Brandy and Wine Vaults, Dove-Tavern, 24, Market-place

Barker Jeremiah, Pawn-Broker, 14, Lower Westwick-str.

Barker Christopher, Wool-pack, 46, Botolph-street

Barker Mary, Weigh-house, 20, Castle Ditches

Barker Thomas, Whitesmith, 13, Red-Lion-lane

Barlow James, Worsted Manufacturer, 9, Timberhill-street

Barlow Robert, Gent. 18, Bethel-street

Barlow John, Shawl-Manufacturer, St. Margaret's Churchyard

Barlow John, Hair-dresser, 12, Magdalen-street

Barnard I. C. 19, Botolph-street

Barnard I. Angier, and Barnards, Merchants, 19, Botolph-street

Barnard Abraham, 41, Botolph-street

Barnard William and Sons, Merchants, 9, Muspole-street

Barnes Philip, Bricklayer, 18, All Saints' Green

Barnham John, Pawn-Broker, 189, King-street

Barrett and Brooks, Curriers and Leather Cutters, 2 and 3, Lower Goat-lane

Barrow Edward, Gent. 13, Pitt-street

Barrow Isaac, Gent. 3, Upper Surry-street, Mews

Barrow and Scott, Cotton-Manufacturers, 50, Colegate street

Barrows Messdms. Tea-Dealers, 5, Briggs' lane

Barton William, Corn and Coal Merchant, 164, King-street

Barwell John, Importer and Dealer in Foreign Wines, &c. 7, St Stephen's street

Barwick George, Gun-Maker, 113, Pottergate-street

Basey Charles, Broker, 15, Soutergate-street

Basham Charles, Appraiser and Auctioneer, St. Stephen's str.

Bassley William, Leather-dresser, 2, Colegate-street

Bates Benjamin, Grocer, &c. 26, Westwick-street

Bath Francis and Co. Stay and Habit makers, 24, Bethel-str.

Bayfield Thomas, Ironmonger, Oil and Colour Man, 32, Magdalen-street

Bayfield Thomas, Baker, 34, Coslany-street

Beane Joseph, Master of Doughty's Hospital, Snailgate street

Beane Robert, Bull's Head, 62, Ber-street

Beare William, Boot and Shoe maker, 11, St. Peter's

Beare Thomas, Currier and Leather Cutter, 26, St. George's Bridge-street

Beare John, Boot and Shoe maker, 27, St. George's Bridge-street

Beatley William, Eating-house, 5, Lower Goat-lane

Beatniffe Richard, Bookseller, Binder, and Stationer, 6, Cockey-lane

Beesley George, Boot and Shoe maker, 7, Coslany-street

Beavor James, Esq. 88, Magdalen-street

Beavor William, Carpenter, &c. 46, St. Stephen's street

Beevor James, Esq. 72, St. Giles's Broad-street

Beevor Rev. John, Willow-lane, St. Giles'

Beevor Henry, 58, St. Giles'

Beckham Edward, Cooper, 9, St. George's Bridge-street

Beckwith Mrs. 6, Lower Close

Beckwith Rev. Thomas, 10, St. Martin's by Palace

Beckwith John, Musician, 25, Lower Close

Bedford Charles, Coppersmith, 6, Pottergate-street

Begg John, Attorney, Surveyor of the Window-Lights, &c. for Yarmouth District, 40, Pottergate-street

Bell Thomas, Carpenter, &c. King street

Bell John, Yarn-Manufacturer, Fishgate-street

Beloe James, Basket-maker, Trowse

Bennett James, Clock and Watch Maker, 2, Briggs' lane

Bensley Edward, 25, Cock, Rampant Horse street

Bensley Robert, Baker, 8, St. Stephen's street

Bensley John, Carpenter, 23, All Saints' Green

Bensley and Dale, Wholesale Linen-Drapers and Haberdashers, 9 and 10, London-lane, and 3, St. Andrew's Steps

Berry and Rochester, Booksellers and Stationers, 11, Dove-lane

Bexfield Richard, Cabinet-maker, at the Goat, 14, Upper Goat-lane

Bidwell Richard, Draper and Hosier, 6, St. George's Bridge-street

Bidwell and Co. Sack-Manufacturers, Colegate street

Bignold Thomas, Brandy, Wine, and Hop Merchant, 18, Market-place

Bird Bailey, Land-Surveyor, Red-Lion-lane

Bird William, Broker, 9, ditto

Bishop's Office, 20, Upper Close—Mr. Charles Kitson, 8, Upper Close, Deputy-Register

Black Thomas, Gent. 3, Upper Close

Black Thomas and William, Confectioners, 1, Hay-market

Blackburn John, Stone and Marble Mason, 3, Castle-Meadow

Blake Thomas, jun. Esq. Barrister at Law, 5, Queen-street

Blake John, House-Steward, 28, Bethel-street

Blake Hammond, Hemp-Cloth Manufacturer, 54, Magdalen-street

Blake Robert, Cotton-Manufacturer, 24, Heigham-street

Blake Isaac, Hotpresser, 35, Snailgate-street

Blake William, Pork-Butcher, 11, Coslany-bridge

Blakley Elijah, Cotton-Manufacturer, Colegate-street

Bland Thomas, Gent. 18, Botolph-street

Bland Michael, Gent. 9, ditto

Blogg Samuel, Lime Burner and Brick Maker, Brick-Ground, Surry road

Bloom D. and Co. Merchants, 2, Duke's Palace, and Trowse Mills

Blowfield, Peter, Carpenter, &c. 52, St. Martin's street

Blyth Samuel, Plasterer, 87, Pottergate-street

Boardman John, Hatter and Hosier, 1, Market-place, and 1, Cockey-lane

Boardman Benjamin, Woollen-Draper, 22, Market-place

Boast Robert, Sawyer, 2, Ber-street

Bokenham Thomas, Surgeon, 10, Upper Westwick-street

Bolingbroke Nathaniel, Silversmith and Haberdasher, 2, Market-place

Bolingbroke J. B. and Co. Woollen-Drapers, 4, St. Peter's

Bolton John, Corn-Merchant, at Staith, 104, King-street, Dwelling-House, 2, St. Faith's lane

Bolton John, 11, Woolpack-Inn, St. Giles's Broad-street

Bolton Ziba, Coach-Master, 14, Hungate-street

Bond William, Surgeon, 8, Tombland

Bond John, Boot and Shoe maker, 46, St. Giles's Broad-str.

Bone Nicholas, Boot and Shoe Maker, 15, Lower Goat-lane

Booth Mrs. Castle Inn, 13, White-Lion-lane

Booth William, Bookseller, &c. 37, Market-place

Booty William, Shopkeeper, 22, King-street

Borking and Carver, Woolcombers, 66, Gildengate street

Borough Stephen, Dolphin Inn, Upper Heigham

Boswell Thomas, at the Canteen, Horse-Barracks

Botwright William, Grocer, 25, St. George's Bridge-street

Boulter Thomas, Baker, 15, St. Giles's Broad-street

Bowen Ann, Stationer, &c. 4, Cockey-lane

Bowles William, Farmer, Eaton, and at the George, St. Stephen's, on Saturdays

Boyce James, Attorney at Law, 11, Wymer-street

Bradford Miles, Boot and Shoe maker, 42, London-lane

Bradford William, Esq. 68, Pottergate-street

Brady John, White-Horse, 98, Magdalen-street

Bradley John, Boot and Shoe maker, 6, Fyebridge-street

Bray John, jun. Tailor, &c. St. Andrew's Bridge-street

Bream Samuel, Gent. 4, Wilkes's lane, near Bank place

Brereton John, Sadler, 33, Upper Westwick street

Bresley Mrs. Oatmeal-maker, St. Simon's

Brett William, Wine and Brandy Merchant, 8, Wastlegate-lane, All Saints

Brett John, Baker, 8, Fishgate-street

Brett Robert, Tailor, &c. 31, London-lane

Brewer Marke, 48, Queen's Head, St. Giles

Brewerton Thomas, Corn-Merchant, Lower Westwick-street

Briggs Cornelius, Millwright, 24, St. Martin's lane

Briggs James, Coal Merchant, 96, Colegate street

Briggs James, Coal-Merchant, White Friar's Bridge

Britton Henry, Clock and Watch maker, 9, Briggs' lane

Britton Richard, New Theatre Inn, 56, Bethel-street

Brooks Richard, Grocer, &c. 32, Coslany street

Brooks John, Dwelling-House, 25, St. Martin's lane

Browne Robert Ives, Esq. 2, Upper Close

Browne John and Son, Ironmongers, Ironfounders, and Colourmen, 4, Upper Market

Browne George, Collector of the Post-Horse Duty, 13, St. Giles'

Browne Arthur, Hatter, &c. 10, Cockey-lane

Browne Christopher, Coal and Corn Merchant and Malster, 122, King-street

Brown Robert, Corn and Coal Merchant, 17, Lower Close

Brown John, Millwright and Ironfounder, Timberhill-street

Browns T. and W. Pipe-makers, 30, All Saints' Green

Browne Thomas, Plumber, &c. 6, Ber street

Browne Elizabeth, Milliner, 61, Bethel-street

Browne Edward, Carpenter, 30, King-street

Browne William, Baker, 59, St. Martin's street

Browne James, Mounter, 41, Pitt-street

Browne John, Lord Nelson's Gardens, Bracondale

Brown Thomas, Black Friars, 1, St. George's Bridge-street

Browne Benjamin, Tailor, 2, St. Clement's Church-yard

Brown Edward, Carpenter, &c. 7, Chancery-street, St. Andrew's

Brown Charles, late at the Castle and Lion, St. Peter's, but now at the Elephant, Magdalen-street

Brown John, Breeches-maker, 9, Dove-lane

Browne George, Pipe-maker, Gapp's Yard, Upper Westwick-street

Browne Mary, House-Broker, 8, Bridewell-Alley

Brunton John, Gent. 2, Theatre-Square

Brunton James, Mace-Officer, 35, St. Giles'

Brunton Mrs. Baker, 8, Hungate-street

Buck Robert, Flour-Merchant, Florden, and at the Rampant-Horse, St. Stephen's, Norwich, on Saturdays

Buck John, Flour Merchant, St. Clement's Hill, and at the King's Head, on Saturdays

Buck John, Miller, 57, St. Stephen's street

Buck John, Wheelwright, St. Benedict's road

Buck Jeremiah, Tailor, &c. Upper Goat-lane

Buckle I. and W. Ironmongers, Tobacconists and Colourmen, 6, Haymaket

Buckenham John, Plumber, 30, St. George's Bridge-street

Buddry Anthony, Grocer and Tea-Dealer, 19, St. Martin's by Palace

Bullard James, Master of Bethel, 46

Bullen Joshua, Ironmonger, &c. 44, Market-place

Bullen Joseph, Tailor, &c. 10, White Lion-lane

Burcham Samuel, Tailor, 15, Lower Close

Burdett John, Bricklayer, 36, Snailgate-street

Burrel Thomas, Importer of Spirits, 120, King-street

Burrel Robert, Gent. 21, Upper Close

Burrel James, Boot and Shoe Maker, 24, Magdalen-street

Burrows William, Grocer, Tea-Dealer, and Tobacconist, 10, ditto

Burrows John, Woolcomber, &c. 21, Barrack-street

Burks John, Silk-Dyer, 6, All Saints', Green—Also a Porter Merchant

Burt William, Upholder, 11, Briggs' lane

Burton Thomas, Esq. Bracondale-hill

Burton John, Black Horse Inn, 7, Tombland

Bush John, Boot and Shoe maker, 5, Magdalen-street

Buttisant Thomas, Hair-Dresser, 9, Tombland

Butterton James, Dyer, 6, Elm-hill street

Buttivant James, Manufacturer, 16, Castle-Meadow

C

Calthorpe Christoper, Cooper, 13, London-lane

Calthorpe Christopher, Cooper, at the Cherry-tree, 51, Gildengate-street

Campin Robert, Linen-Draper, &c. 2, Cockey-lane

Candler Lawrence and Son, Flour-Merchants, Cringleford, and at the Rampant-Horse, St. Stephen's, on Saturdays

Candler Benjamin, Grocer and Tea-Dealer, 8, Little Cockey lane

Cann James, Cabinet-maker, 35, Timberhill-street

Cannel John, Collar and Harness Maker, 3, St. Stephen's str.

Capon Christopher, Painter, &c. 47, Colegate-street

Capon Christopher, jun. Painter, 37, Bethel-street

Carr William, Boot and Shoe Maker, 59, Coslany-street

Carr William, Boot and Shoe Maker, 26, Botolph-street

Carr Francis, Shoe-maker, 7, St. Augustine's street

Carman John, Umbrella-maker, 2, Wastlegate-street, All Saints'

Carter Samuel, Pelican, 2, Pitt-street

Carter J. G. Corn-Merchant, Windham, and at the Coach-makers' Arms, St. Stephen's Road, on Saturdays

Carter Joseph, Master-Weaver, 77, St. Giles'

Carter Mary, Broker, 26, Rampant Horse-street

Carter William, Esq. Collector of the Excise, Sampson and Hercules' Court, Tombland

Carver Mrs. 25, St. Giles'

Carver Daniel, Stuff Manufacturer, 13, Timberhill-street

Catchpole John, Hair-Dresser, 6, Briggs' lane

Cattermoul Thomas and Son, Wine-Merchants, 1, Red-Well street

Caxton Henry, Innkeeper, 33, Market-place

Challis John, Boot and Shoe maker, 2, Pudding-lane

Chalker Noah, 10, Coach and Horses, Red-Lion-lane

Chambers N. Surgeon, 5, Chapel-field

Chamberlin Peter and Son, Grocers, Tallow-Chandlers, and Tea-Dealers, 1, Upper Market

Chamberlin Charles, Orange-Merchant, 9, White-Lion-lane

Chamberlin Peter, Linen and Woollen Draper, 23, White-Lion-lane

Chamberlin James, Shopkeeper, 59, King-street

Chamberlin Henry, Shopkeeper, 26, St. Augustine's street

Chamberlin George, Carpenter, &c. Trowse

Chaplin William, Writing-Master, 17, Pottergate-street

Chapman Rev. 59, ditto

Chapman Gardiner, Attorney, 9, Upper Close

Chapman Spinks, Wine-Vaults, 7, Market-Place

Chapman William George, jun. 15, Hay-market

Chapman Samuel, Baker, 35, Botolph-street

Chapman James, Hempen Cloth Manufacturer, Bungay, and in Weaver's lane, Norwich, on Saturdays

Charlesworth Joseph, Duffield Manufacturer, 58, Coslany-str.

Chase James, Importer and Dealer in Foreign Spirits, 29, King-str

Chesnutt Ann, Sadler, &c. 4, Bridge street, St. George's

Chesnutt Ann, Harness Maker, 28, Magdalen-street

Chettleburgh Robert, Haberdasher, Hosier, and Cutler, 8, Hay Market

Chettleburgh William, Baker, 23, Rampant-Horse street

Chettleburgh Daniel, Sadler, 201, King-street

Chettleburgh Harrison, Plumber, 7, Queen-street

Chipperfield Robert, Half-Moon, Market-place

Chittock William, Tailor, Stay and Habit Maker, 14, Red Lion-lane

Christian Edward, Dancing-Master, 11, Red-Well street

Churchman John, Esq. 12, St. Faith's lane

Clabourn William, Hosier, 71, St. Stephen's street

Clabburn William, Hosier, 26, Timberhill-street

Clabburn John, Confectioner, 11, Fyebridge-street

Clabburn Robert, Woolcomber, 2, St. Simon's

Clarke and Watts, Warehousemen, 3, Chapel-field-lane

Clarke George, Fish-monger, 15, Fish-market

Clarke Daniel, Coal-Merchant, 12, Lower Close

Clarke William, Boot and Shoe Maker, 2, Dove-lane

Clarke John, Black-Bull Inn, 11, Magdalen-street

Clarke Ephraim, Boot and Shoe Maker, 20, ditto

Clarke Robert, Boot and Shoe Maker, 2, Gildengate-street

Clarke William, Kitteringham, and at the Angel, Norwich, on Saturdays

Clary William, Coach-Makers' Arms, 4, St. Stephen's road

Claxon John, Lodging-House, St. Stephen's Church-yard

Clemment's Francis and Co. Coach-Makers, 7, Back of the Inns

Clift Levold, Throwsterer, 11, Lower Close

Clover Joseph, Gent, 33, Coslany-street

Clover Joseph, jun. 40, Snailgate street

Clowes Mrs. 1, Rampant Horse street

Clowting Henry, 5, Black Prince in Butchery, Market-place

Cock Joseph, Wine-Merchant, 12, Timberhill-street

Cock and Pitchers, Importers of Wine and Foreign Spirits, 7, White-Lion-lane

Cocksel John, Three Dyers, 67, Lower Westwick-street

Coe John, Broker, 9, Upper Westwick-street

Coes' (Miss) Boarding-School, 1, Griffin-lane

Coggle William, Shopkeeper, 16, Rosemary-lane

Cogman Benjamin, Baker, 19, Ber-street

Coke Jacob, Vinegar Maker, in Court, St. Giles'

Cole John Hammond, 71, Stamp-Office, St. Giles'

Coles and Co. Wholesale Drapers and Haberdashers, 18, White Lion-lane

Coleby James, Boot and Shoe Maker, 7, St. Peter's

Coleby Samuel, Gardner, 33, Magdalen-street

Colkett Mrs. Druggist, 70, St. Stephen's street

Coleman John, Builder, Coslany-street

Coleman George, Bricklayer, 18, St. Martin's street

Collins David, Boot and Shoe Maker, 12, Lower Westwick-street

Colls William, King's Head, 116, Magdalen-street

Collumbine Peter and Sons, Merchants, 1, St. Simon's

Colman Edward, Surgeon, 12, Tombland

Colombine Paul, D.D. 10, Tombland

Colombine David, Esq. 15, Upper Close

Cone Samuel, Throwsterer, Norman's lane

Connel James, Smith, Trowse

Cook Samuel, Hotpresser, 4 and 5, Peacock-street

Cook George, Esq. 1, St. Gregory's Church-yard

Cooke Thomas, Esq. 22, Tombland

Cooke William, Grocer, 52, Bridge-street, St. George's

Cooper Mrs. 202, King-street

Cooper Charles, Gent. 48, Lower Westwick street

Cooper Lewis and Co. Linen-Drapers, 50, Market-place

Cooper Robert, Shopkeeper, 3, Magdalen-street

Cooper Robert, Shopkeeper, 71, Gildengate-street

Coote Thomas, Ironmonger, 8 and 9, Bank-place, and 1 Queen-street

Copeman E. and R. Woollen-Drapers, 48, Market-place

Copeman Edward, Dwelling-House, 54, St. Giles'

Coppin James, Plumber, &c. 20, Hay-market

Coppin Daniel, Painter and Gilder, 6, St Stephen's street

Copping Mrs. Baker, 62 Upper Westwick street

Coppin Miss, Milliner, 39, Snailgate-street

Corbould John, Esq. 65, St. Giles'

Cordran Edward, White Swan, 16, Upper Market

Corfield Elizabeth, Leather-Cutter, 14, Hog-hill

Corke William, Plumber, &c. 52, Upper Westwick street

Cossey Thomas, Bakers' Arms, 5, Ber street

Cotman Edmund, Haberdasher and Hosier, 18, Cockey-lane

Cotton Elizabeth, White-Hart Inn, St. Peter's

Coulsen Ralph, Wool Factor, 7, Muspole-street

Coushen Samuel, White Swan, 28, King street

Cousins John, Leather-Cutter, 3, Upper Market

Cox Daniel, Smith, 19, Fyebridge-street

Cozens John, Grocer and Tea-Dealer, 12, Market-place

Crabtree Grenville, Farmer, Witton, and at the Baker's Arms, Ber-street, on Saturdays

Crake Mary, Saleshop, 7 and 9, St. Andrew's Plain

Crackenthorpe Samuel, Gent. 73, St. Stephen's street

Craske Peter, Boot and Shoe Maker, 7, St. Gregory's Church Yard

Craske Christopher, Baker, 48, St. Martin's street

Creasey and Page, Salesmen, 4, St. Andrew's Plain

Creed Matthew, White Lion, 23, St. Martin's by Palace Plain

Cripps George, Grocer and Tea-Dealer, 40, Market-place

Critchfield James, Working-Cutler and Hardwareman, 21, Market-place

Crockett Sarah, Stationer, 17, Fyebridge-street

Crome John, Drawing Master, 17, Gildengate-street

Cropley Richard, Boot and Shoe Maker, 34, Snailgate-street

Cross Joseph, Patten-Maker, 12, Rampant-Horse street

Crotch Michael, Organ Builder, 1, Green's lane, St. George's

Crowe James, Esq. Lakenham

Crowe William, Worsted-Manufacturer, 9, Pitt-street

Crowe Spicer, Plumber, 89, Upper Westwick street

Cruttenden William Courtney, Esq. 12, St. Saviour's lane

Culley Richard and Co. Grocers and Salt-Merchants, 14, Upper Market

Culley John, Cabinet and Chair Maker, 43, London-lane

Culling William, Working-Cutler, 39, Market-place

Cullington James, Prussia Gardens, St. Stephen's road

Cullington Robert, Hair-Dresser, 2, Timberhill

Cullyer John, Whitesmith, 6, Cow-hill

Culyer William, Cooper, 27, Rampant-Horse-street

Culyer William, licensed to let Post-Horses, Wool-Pack-yard, St. Giles'

Culyer Samuel, Boot and Shoe Maker, 25, Timberhill-street

Cupper Thomas, Brewer, Corn and Coal Merchant, 134, Magdalen-street

Curtis John, Exhibitor of Natural Curiosities, 2, Castle-Ditches

Cushing Samuel, Carver and Gilder, 9, Broad-street, St. Giles'

Cushing John, Bookbinder, 8, Lady's lane

Cushing Joshua, Stone-Mason, St. Andrew's Bridge street

Cutler Thomas, Upholder, 8, Dove-lane

Cutten William, Esq. 117, Magdalen-street

D

Dady George, Timber-Merchant, Imperial Arms, 12, King-street

Dady Charles, Eating House, 14, Bridewell-Alley

Daines William, Shopkeer, 84, Magdalen street

Dale John, Hair-Dresser, 4, Bethel-street

Dalrymple William, Surgeon, 40, Colegate-street

Dalrymple John, Brandy-Merchant, 13, Back of the Inns

Damant Francis, Harness-Maker, 118, Magdalen-street

Danton Joseph, Red Lion, 13, London lane

Darby John, Whitesmith, 8, Cross lane, St. George's street

Darby William, Turner, 14, Rosemary lane

Darby Robert, Wheelwright, Trowse

Darkin Robert, Broker, 2, Red-Lion-lane

Darkin George, Broker, 120, Pottergate-street

Daveney Charles, Grocer and Tea-Dealer, 9, Cockey-lane

Davey Jonathan, Esq. 27, Upper Westwick street

Davey Robert, Clock and Watch Maker, 6, Back of the Inns

Davis John, Gent. Ladies' Row, St. Stephen's road

Dawson and Leeds, Scarlet-Dyers, 5, St. Clement's Churchyard

Day Thomas, Esq. 12, St. Martin's Plain

Day Rev. Richard, 92, Pottergate-street

Day John, Woolcomber, St. George's Bridge street

Day William, Eating-House, 16, St. Stephen's street

Daydon John, Gent. 35, Cowgate-street

Daynes Mrs. Milliner, 77, Magdalen-street

Daynes Samuel, Basket-Maker, 23, Hay-market

Deacon Rev. John, 19, St. Martin's lane

Deakin Rev. Thomas, 70, St Giles'

Dean and Chapter's Office, 30, Lower Close square—Mr. William Utten, Clerk and Register

Deans James, Corn and Coal Merchant, 32, Wymer-street

De Carle Robert, Stone-Mason, 13, Wymer-street

Deday Thomas, Manufacturer, 49, Coslany-street

Denew Peter, Farmer, Hetherset, and at the George, Hay-market, on Saturdays

De Hague Elisha, Attorney, 5, Elm hill-street

Delf Thomas, Tuns' Tavern, Cooper's Court, Cockey-lane

Delight and Son, Boot and Shoe Makers, 2, White-Lion-lane

Delph Moses, Whitesmith, 5, Little Rampant Horse street

Denham Samuel, Boot and Shoe Maker, 11, Coslany street

Denmark Thomas, Glover, &c. 19, Back of the Inns

Denny Martin, Boot and Shoe Maker, 90, Upper Westwick-street

Devereux Edmund, Plumber, &c. 73 and 4, Gildengate-str.

Dexter Matthew and Co. Hosiers and Lace-Manufacturers, 3, Back of the Inns

Dickerson Daniel, Watch-Maker, 9, St. Martin's by Palace

Digby John, Greyhound, 33, Surry-street.

Dilley John, Catharine Wheel, 19, St. Augustine's street

Dingle John, Throwsterer, 37, Botolph-street

Dingle John, jun. Shawl-Manufacturer, 38, Botolph-street

Dinmore Richard, Gent. 20, Timberhill-street

Ditchell Anthony, Esq. 86, Pottergate-street

Dix William, Shoe-Maker, 26, ditto

Dixon Daniel, Hair-Dresser, 22, Hay-market

Dixon Futter, Shoulder of Mutton, 30, St. Stephen's street.

Dobson James, Carpenter, 6, Upper Surry street

Dove Susannah, Hat-Maker, 2, Upper Market

Dove Thomas, Carpenter, 4, Scole's Green

Doyley Henry, Hempnall, Hempen-Cloth Manufacturer, and in Weaver's lane, on Saturdays

Drakes Miss, Boarding-School, 31, All Saints' Green

Drake Robert, White-Horse Inn, 2, Hay-market

Drake Francis, Cooper, 11, St. Martin's by Palace

Drake Richard, Cabinet-Maker, 2, St. Andrew's, Chancery-street

Dring George, Baker, 49, Magdalen-street

Dring John, Baker, 31, St. Giles'

Drummond Rev. Thomas, 200, King-street

Duckett Sarah, King's Head, 25, St. Stephen's street

Duckett John, Hair-Dresser, 43, Coslany-street

Duckett William, Old Church Stile, 26, Upper Market

Dunham and Yallop, Goldsmiths and Tea-Dealers, 10, Market-place

Dunn Jeremiah, Tailor, &c. Lamb-Inn yard, Hay-market

Dunn George, Three Cranes, 21, Lower Close square

Dunn James, Boot and Shoe Maker, 1, Alms-lane

Dunn John, Baker, 27, Pottergate street

Durrant James, Queen Ann, 17, Colegate-street

Durrant Thomas, Shopkeeper, 20, Heigham-street

Durrant Thomas, Buck, 43, St. Martin's street

Dyball Thomas, Baker, 74, Magdalen-street

Dye Isaac, Grocer and Tea-Dealer, 53, St. Stephen's street

Dye James, Fishmonger, 16, Fish-market

Dye Thomas, Coach-Master, 13, St. Martin's by Palace

Dyson William, at the Cow, Cow-hill street

Dyson Joseph, Dyer, Charlotte-yard, St. Stephen's

E

Earl Elden, Chair and Cabinet Maker, 13, Rampant-Horse street

Estaugh Nathaniel, Bellman, 39, Bethel-street

Eaton Thomas, Silk-Mercer, 3, Market-place

Ecclestone Richard, Currier, &c. 14, Wymer-street

Edgar William, Fishmonger, 20, Fishmarket

Edwards W. C. Engraver and Drawing-Master, 32, London, lane

Edwards Samuel, Hair-Dresser, 68, St. Stephen's

Edwards William, Glover, &c. Goodman's Court, St. Stephen's

Edwards William, Tailor and Draper, 13, Hog-hill

Edwards John, Carpenter, 3, St. Margaret's Church-yard

Edwards Edward, Gardner, 5, ditto

Edwards John, Baker, 25, St Augustine's street

Eldred John, White Lion, 44, Upper Westwick street

Elliott John, Sadler, Ironmonger, 1, London-lane

Ellis John, Gent. 20, Lower Close

Elmer Joseph, Throwster, 7, St. Clement's Church-yard

Elwin Thomas, Esq. 5, Fyebridge-street

Elwin Marsham, Gent. 5, Upper Close

Elwin James, Baker, 45, Pottergate-street

Elwin Mrs. 3, Golden-Dog lane

English James, Writing-Master, 87, Upper Westwick street

English Joseph, Woolcomber, 14, St. Margaret's Churchyard

English John, Turner, &c. 21, St. Stephen's street

Evans T. B. Esq. 4, Little Rampant-Horse street

F

Fair Charles, Boot and Shoe Maker, 5, Gildengate-street

Fairhead Charles, Bricklayer, 16, St. Martin's by Palace str.

Fellows Samuel, Leather-Cutter, 25, Wymer-street

Fenn Abraham, Boot and Shoe-maker, 20, Tombland

Fiddey Henry, Broker, 11, Hog-hill

Fiddey John, Butcher, 1, Butchery-market

Field Elizabeth, Glover, 7, St. Giles'

Finch Peter, Brewer, 41, Coslany-street

Firman William, Baker, 38, Ber-street

Fish Thomas, Cabinet-Maker, &c. 4, Bridewell Alley

Fish John, Shawl and Cotton Manufacturer, Fish-gate street

Fisher George, Tailor, 15, St. Stephen's road

Fiske Hammond, Deal, Timber Merchant, and Builder, Fishgate-street

Fitt William, Carpenter, 8, Golden Ball lane

Flegg Edward, Schoolmaster, 10, St. Martin's lane

Fletcher Thomas, Cord and Rope Maker, 4, Dove-lane

Flint Richard, Sack-Manufacturer, Colegate-street

Folliot John, Shopkeeper, 95, Pottergate-street

Foster, Son, Unthank, and Forster, Attorneys, 11, Queen-street

Forster William, Attorney, 6, Little Rampant-Horse street

Foster, Dwelling-House, 15, Castle-Meadow

Forster D. D. Master of the Free Grammar School, Upper-Close

Forster Charles, Plumber and Glazier, 20, King-street

Forster and Waite, Coppersmiths and Braziers, 2, Broad-street, St. Giles'

Forster Richard, Esq. Eaton

Foster John, Bowl-Turner, Trowse

Fort Thomas, Shopkeeper, 12, St George's Bridge-street

Foulger William, Flour-Merchant, Trowse

Foulsham Mrs. 32, St. Stephen's road

Foulsham and Nave, Builders, 3, Chapel-field

Fountain Martin, Bricklayer, 10, Tooley-street

Fox John, Plumber, &c. 125, Pottergate-street

Fox William, Engineer to the Water-Works, 44, Lower Westwick street

Francis Samuel, Woolcomber, 8, St. Martin's by Palace str.

Francis Mrs. Register-Office, 4, Surry-street

Freeman Jeremiah, Carver, Gilder, and Printseller, 2, London-lane

Freeman R. H. Tailor and Salesman, 11 and 13, St. George's Bridge-street

Freeman Mrs. Throwsterer, 29, Snailgate-street

Freeman John, Cabinet-Maker and Upholder, 11 and 12, Upper-Market

Freeman Edward, Cabinet-Maker, 16, Back of the Inns

Freeman James, Throwsterer, Stepping-lane, near King-str.

Freshfield John, Hop-Merchant, 3, Elm-hill-street

French John, Hair-Dresser, 28, St. George's Bridge street

Frewer and Son, Sadlers, 11, Hay-market

Fromantel Daniel, Manufacturer, 3, in Court, Chapel-field-lane

Frost Mrs. St. Giles's road

Frost James, Builder, 41, St. Stephen's street

Fulcher James, Brush-Maker, 10, Hay-market

Futter John, Farmer, Ketteringham, and at the Angel, on Saturdays

G

Ganning Daniel, Gent. 23, St. Giles'

Gapp James, Merchant, 8, Coslany Bridge-street

Gapp James, Dyer, 60, Coslany-street

Gardiner Richard, Corn-Merchant, 138, King-street

Gardiner Michael, Salesman, 5, St. Andrew's Plain

Gardiner Thomas, Throwsterer, 2, Soutergate-street

Garland Thomas, Esq. 5, Lower Close

Gatley David, Woolcomber, 14, St. Andrew's Bridge-street

Gay Robert, Basket-Maker, 15, Tombland

Gaze John, Tanner, 11, Heigham street

Gaze Thomas, Stationer and Broker, 17, Red Lion-lane

Gaze Samuel, Three Compasses, 203, King-street

Gee Benjamin, Crown and Anchor, 29, Gildengate-street

Geldart Joseph and Son, Wine-Merchants, 15, Fyebridge-str.

Geldart Joseph, jun. 2, Fyebridge-street

Gibson Joseph, Master Weaver, 18, St Martin's by Palace Plain

Gibson David, Tailor, 15, Bridewell-Alley

Gibbs William, Throwsterer, 4, Barrack-street

Gidney James, Fruiterer, 11, Red-Lion-lane

Gidney John, Fruiterer, 10, Queen-street

Gidney Jeremiah, Master of the Boys' Hospital

Gifford Christopher, Broker, 31, Timberhill-street

Gillman Mrs. Haberdasher, 46, London-lane

Gilman Thomas, Linen-Draper and Haberdasher, 24 Cockey-lane

Gilmer David, Broker, 15 and 16, Maddermarket-street

Gilmore William, Boot and Shoe Maker, 4, Magdalen-street

Gilney Christopher, Cabinet-Maker, 40, Castle-Ditches

Glover Rev. Edward, 91, Pottergate-street

Goal William, Duffield-Maker, 17, St. Martin's street

Godfry Ann, Milliner, 45, Market-place

Godfrey Sarah, Linen-Draper, 20, Market-place

Golden Frederick, Baker, 184, King-street

Gooch C. Bricklayer, Trowse

Gooch Henry, Yarn-Factor, 9, Maddermarket-street

Goodwin Sibias, Liquor-Merchant, 1, Pudding-lane

Goodwin James, Attorney, 2, Gun-lane

Goodwin Peter, Baker, 27, Wymer street

Goodwin John, Throwsterer, 5, St. Saviour's lane

Goose R. Horse Dealer, 31, St. Stephen's road

Gordon Rev. William, 6, St. Faith's lane

Gordon Capt. 21, Hungate-street

Gosnold Mary, Tailor, &c. 8, St. Giles's Broad street

Goss John, Dyer, Elm-hill street

Gostling Francis, Merchant, 3, Duke's Palace

Gostling Francis, Vinegar Yard, 7, St. Faith's lane

Gostling Edward, Plumber 5, Wymer street

Gotts George, Smith and Farrier, 5, St. Augustine's street

Goulty Richard, Boot and Shoe Maker, 10, Back of the Inns

Gowen Thomas, Licensed to Let Post Horses, 23, Bethel str.

Graham W. G. Haberdasher, 8, Cockey-lane

Graham George, Glover, &c. 10, Upper Market

Grand John, Attorney, at Mr. Capon's, 37, Bethel-street

Grant Charles, Tailor and Habit Maker, 27, Tombland

Grant Mrs. Matron at the Hospital

Graver Mountain, Lobster Inn, 24, Pottergate street

Graves Jeremiah, Woollen Draper, 9, Market-place

Graves John and Co. Hotpressers, 16, Tooley street

Gray Robert, Cabinet Maker, 22, Wymer street

Green Ann, Butcher, 8, Fishmarket

Green James, Boot and Shoe Maker, 15, Red Lion lane

Green John, Horse-Dealer, 7, Wastlegate lane, All Saints

Green William, Carpenter, 80, Lower Westwick street

Green John, Bricklayer, 38, Colegate street

Green J. B. Carpenter, Tooley street

Green James, Wroxham, Gent. and at J. Green's, Bricklayer, Colegate street, on Saturdays

Greenfield Thomas, Jolly Farmers, 3, Castle Ditches

Gridley H. Woolcomber, 190, King street

Grienfield Daniel, Baker, 18, Golden Ball lane

Grinling James, Woollen Draper, 41, London lane

Grimmer Thomas Carpenter, 18, St. Martin's lane

Gunton James, Cabinet and Chair Maker, 4, Timberhill str.

Gurney Mrs. Haberdasher, 11, Rampant Horse street

Gurney Richard, Bartlett and Joseph, Bankers, 1, Bank Place

Gurney Bartlett, Esq. 2, Bank Place

Gurney Hudson, Esq. Queen's street

Gurney Joseph, Esq. at the Grove, St. Stephen's

Gurney, Webb, and Son, Wool and Yarn Factors, 1, Coslany street

Gurney Samuel, 18, Red Lion lane.

H

Hadman James, Sun and Anchor Tavern, 19, Pottergate str.

Haggard William, Esq. 8, Wymer street

Hall Henry, Gent. 139, Ber street

Hall Samuel, Boot and Shoe Maker, 32, Pottergate street

Hall Thomas, Dyer, 17, Fishgate street

Hammond William, Gent. 46, Pottergate street

Hammond Joseph, Long Stratton, and at Tuck's Coffee-House, Norwich

Hampp Christopher, Master Weaver, 20, St. Giles'

Hancock Rev. Thomas, 2, Bishopsgate street

Hancock James, Gent. 26, Bethel-street

Hanmant William, Coal Merchant, 97, King-street

Hansell Rev. 10, Upper Close

Hanworth John, Boot and Shoe Maker, 13, Bethel street

Hanks William, jun. Merchant, 31, Colegate-street

Hanks William, Merchant, 26, Colegate-street

Hardy George, Apothecary, at the Hospital

Hardy James and Son, Grocers and Tea-Dealers, 19, Rampant-Horse street

Harcourt William, Hatter, Hosier, and Draper, 7, Hay-market

Harling Benjamin, Baker, 2, Bethel-street

Harmer William, Coal Merchant, 50, St. Stephen's street

Harmer Henry, Attorney, 6, Chapel-field-lane

Harmer Samuel, Attorney, 6, Chapel-field-lane

Harman Richard, Milliner, 20, White Lion-lane

Harman James, Tailor, &c. 1, Wymer-street

Harmar Rebecca, Milliner, St. Margaret's-lane

Harper John, Hatter and Hosier, 7, Cockey-lane

Harper William, Hatter and Hosier, 45, London-lane

Harper William, Plumber, Glazier, and Painter, 26, St. Stephen's street

Harrington John, Butcher, 6, Fish-market

Hart William, Cabinet and Chair Maker, 15, Hog-hill, and 1, Orford-street

Hart Robert, Patten-maker, 7, Lower Westwick-street

Hart Philip, Carpenter, &c. 1, Botolph-street

Harvey Robert, Esq. 31, Surry-street

Harvey Robert, Baker, 4, Ber-street

Harvey and Hudson, Bankers, 198, King-street

Harvey Mrs. G. 6, Bank-Place

Harvey Thomas, Esq. Catton

Harvey Jeremiah, Ives, Esq. Catton

Harvey Robert, Esq. Merchant, 48, Colegate-street

Harwin William, Ironmonger and Colourman, 19, Hog-hill, and Writing Master, 1, Rose-lane

Hatch Richard, Baker, 53, St. Martin's street

Hatch William, Trunk-Maker, 6, Little Cockey-lane

Hawkins Thomas, Grocer, 9, Queen street, and 28, Tombland

Haws John, Boot and Shoe Maker, and Leather Cutter, 20, Back of the Inns

Hawes John, Coach Maker, 13, Hungate-street

Hawsham John, at the Arabian Horse, 2, St. Martin's at Oak street

Haylett Michael, Gardner, at the Pine Apple, 20, St. Martin's at Oak lane

Hayton Mark, Baker, 6, Upper Market

Heald Henry, Gardner, &c. 13, Rose-lane

Heasell John, Cheesemonger, 18, Hay-market

Heasell Thomas, Woolfactor, 2, Red Well-street

Heasell Thomas, Baker, 67, Gildengate-street

Heigham Richard, Linen Draper, 16, Cockey-lane

Henshaw, Steelyard and Scale-Beam Maker, 20, Golden Ball-lane

Herring Robert, Esq. Bracondale hill

Herring John and Sons, Merchants, 63 and 64, Gildengate-str.

Herring John, jun. Esq. Residence, 4, Colegate-street

Herring James, Woollen-Draper, 5, Hay-market

Herring William, Esq. Merchant, 4, St. Faith's lane

Hewett Coleby, Boot and Shoe Maker, 12, Red Lion-lane

Hewett John, Hair Dresser, 29, Magdalen-street

Hibgame Rev. Edward, l, Muspole street

Hickling's (Miss) Boarding School, 8, Chancery street, St. Andrew's

Higgin Christopher, Shawl Manufacturer, 18, Coslany street

Higgin and Clarke, Woolcombers and Worsted Manufacturers, 18, Coslany street

Hill Mary, Baker, 50 and 51, Upper Westwick-street

Hilling William, Confectioner, 6 and 7, Lower Goat-lane

Hilton George, Prince of Wales, 83, Upper Westwick-street

Hodgson James, Ladies' Academy, 6, Wymer-street

Hodgson Charles, Boarding School, 47, Wymer-street

Hogg Edward, Working Cutler, 13, Little Cockey-lane

Holland Samuel, Duffield Maker, 24, Barrack-street

Holland William, Coal Merchant, St. George's Bridge-street

Hollows Thomas, Hair-Dresser, 48, Coslany street

Holmes Thomas, Shopkeeper, 34, King-street

Holmes William, Tailor, 3, St. Gregory's Church-yard

Holt Thomas, Tailor, &c. 14, Peacock-street

Hook Edward, Esq. 59, St. Giles'

Horne Francis, Confectioner, 122, Pottergate-street

Horstead Thomas, Boot and Shoe Maker, 15, Back of the Inns

Horth John, Upholder, 17, White Lion-lane

Houghton Mrs. 2, Griffin-lane

Houghton Henry, Ship-builder, Thorpe

Houghton Robert, Butcher, 3, Hall's End

Howard Adam, White Lion, 36, Bethel-street

Howard John, Baker, 21, Cowgate street

Howard Samuel, Carpenter, &c. 24, Coslany street

Howe John, at the Bear Inn, Market-place

Howell Henry, Hair-Dresser, 1, Castle Ditches

Howes Rev. 2, Cow-Hill

Howes Gordon, Esq. 53, Pottergate-street

Howes William, Hair-Dresser, 17, Hay-market

Howlett James, Wheelwright, &c. 40, St. Martin's at Oak str.

Hubbard William, Fancy Chair-Maker, 12, Broad street, St. Giles'

Hubbard Charles, Linen Draper, &c. 21, White Lion-lane

Hubbard Robert, China and Glass Warehouse, 6, White Lion lane

Hubbard and Wade, Boot and Shoe Makers, 7, Briggs' lane

Hubbard James, Cabinet Maker, 12, St. Andrew's Bridge str.

Hubbard James, Baker, 17, St. Martin's lane

Hubby Simon, House-Broker, 11, Colegate-street

Huggins John, Currier, &c. St. Benedict's road

Hugman Benjamin, Tanner, &c. 13, Heigham street

Humphrey Rev. Richard, Thorpe

Hunnock Henry, Circulating Library, 12, Bridewell Alley

Hunt John, Circulating Library, 12, Red-Well street

Hunt John, Worsted Manufacturer, 45, Gildengate-street

Hutchinson Samuel, Baker, 7, Timberhill-street

Hyde John, Esq. Thorpe

I

Isaac Joseph, Grocer, 5, Chapel-street

Ives Jeremiah, Esq. Mayor, Catton

Ives J. J. and Son, and Basely, Merchants, St. Saviour's Church-lane

Ives Jeremiah, Esq. 1, Colegate-street, and in Town Close

Ives Mrs. 17, Surry street

Ives Mrs. 3, Cook's lane, King-street

Ivory Thomas, Esq. 1, Bishopsgate-street,

Ivory John, Stone Mason, 13, King-street

J

Jacob and Co. Tobacconists, 23, Upper Market

Jackson, Stewardson and Harper, Manufacturers, 56, St. Stephen's street

Jackson William, House Broker, 16, Hog-hill

James John, Glass and China Warehouse, 27, Market-place

James William, Throwsterer, 11, Cowgate-street

Jary William, South Walsham, and at the Angel, Norwich, on Saturdays

Jay Joseph, Coal Merchant and Fishmonger, 19, Coslany street

Jay Thomas and Son, Coal Merchants, 137, King-street

Jay Charles, Fishmonger, 19, Fish-market

Jeckell Thomas, Corn and Coal Merchant, 127, Magdalen-street

Jenner Henry, Draper, Mercer, &c. 2, Hay-market

Jermy William, Felmonger, Dwelling house, Lower Westwick street. Offices at Sandland's Ferry, and St Martin's at Oak

Johnson Lewis, Hair-Dresser, 41, Market-place

Johnson Isaac, Hat-Maker, 8, London-lane

Johnson Mrs. 2, Cook's lane, King street

Johnson John, Patten Maker, 4, St. Martin's by Palace

Johnson Benjamin, Grocer, &c. Upper Westwick-street

Johnson Robert, at the Shell-Work, Heigham

Jones George, Hair-Dresser, 6, Gun-lane

Joslin Robert, Sadler, &c. 7, Madder-market-street

Joy Matthew, Linen-Draper and Haberdasher, 3, White-Lion lane

K

Keer John, Duffield Manufacturer, 9, St Martin's street

Kemp John, Swardestone, and at the Angel, Norwich, on Saturdays

Kent Henry, Boot and Shoe Maker, 22, White-Lion-lane

Keith Christopher, Linen-Draper, 19, Cockey-lane

Kerrison Sir Roger, Knt. and Co. Bankers and Merchants, 8, Back of the Inns

Kerrison John, Ladies' Shoe Maker, 61, St. Giles'

Kett and Back, Bankers, 2, Hog-hill

Kett John, Butcher, 115, Ber-street

Kett John, Butcher, 2, Butchery-Market

Kett Mary, Butcher, 12, Fish-market

Kett Edward, Butcher and Fishmonger, 14, Fishmarket

Kettle James, Mahogany and Deal Merchant, 1, St. Ann's Staith, King-street

Keymer James, Surgeon, 5, Bethel street

Keymer and Baker, Shawl Manufacturers, 22, Magdalen street

Keymer John, Rose Inn, 2, St. Augustine's

Kidd William, Grocer and Tea-Dealer, 4, Elm Hill-street

Kiddell Thomas, Shopkeeper, 11, St. Martin's at Oak street

King Ann, Milliner, &c. 41, Cowgate-street

King James, Throwsterer, 2, St. Swithin's lane

King George, Sadler, 14, White Lion lane

King Thomas, Carpenter, 7, Cow hill

King Samuel, Yarn Factor, 50, Colegate street

Kinnebrook David, School Master, 1, St. Peter's

Kitson Roger, Writing Master, 3, St. Andrew's Plain

Kittle Trivet, Tailor, 20, London-lane

Kittle Richard, Woollen Draper, 25, ditto

Kitton Robert, Grocer, &c. 52, Coslany street

Knights Thomas, Tailor, 1, St. Lawrence Church-yard

Knights John, Tailor, &c. 21, Wastlegate-street, All Saints

Knights, Shawl Manufacturer, Market-place

L

Ladbrook Robert, Drawing Master, 5, Surry street

Ladbrooke Mary, 5, St. Stephen's street

Ladley Thomas, jun. Hempen-Cloth Manufacturer, 52, Lower Westwick-street

Ladley Francis, Shawl Manufacturer, 38, Lower Westwick street

Lamb Thomas, Butcher, 32, Market-place

Lamb Elizabeth, Butcher, 4, Fish-market

Lamb Susannah, Butcher, 5, Fish-market

Lamb John, Butcher, 13, Fish-market

Lamb William, Butcher, 2, Hall's End

Lambert Charles, Stay-Maker, 20, Bethel-street

Lambert Ann, Circulating Library, 1, Back of the Inns

Land Matthew, Butcher, 2, Fish-market

Landy and Fitch, Chymists, &c. 46, Market-place

Landy James, Gent. 68, St. Giles'

Lane Nicholas, Woolcomber, 3, Upper Surry-street

Lane William, Stone Mason, 144, Ber-street

Lane Robert, Broker, 92 and 93, Upper Westwick street

Larke John, Star Inn, 9, Hay-market

Larrance Samuel, Upholder, &c. 1, St. Andrew's Plain

Larter Thomas, Pawnbroker, 28, Wymer-street

Larter Daniel, at the Jolly Gardners, in the Old King's Head Court, St. Stephen's street

Larwood Michael, Cow Keeper, St Stephen's street

Lathom Henry, Esq. 8, Upper Surry-street

Lathom Francis, Esq. 15, St. Martin's by Palace street

Lawne Benjamin, Tailor, 84, St. Giles'

Lawne Sarah, Stay Maker, 40, Bethel-street

Laws Charles, Shopkeeper, 2, St George's Bridge-street

Laws Edward, Gent. 173, King street

Laws William, Waggon and Horses, 3, St Giles' Broad str.

Lawter Joshua, Under Chamberlain, 52, Bethel-street

Layden Ann, Butcher, 3, Fish-market

Lay Charles, Attorney, 40, St. Giles'

Lea James, Waggon and Horses Inn, 13, Tombland

Leach William, King's Head Inn, 11, Market-place

Leeds Charles, 11, Nag's Head Inn, Rampant Horse-street

Leeds Thomas, Oval-Frame Turner, 2, Elm hill-street

Leeds Edward, Brush Maker, and Importer of Foreign Spirits, &c. &c. 123, Pottergate-street

Leeds John, Coal Merchant, 30, Wymer-street

Leeds Stephen, Tanner, Whitwell, and at the Angel, Norwich, on Saturdays

Leggett John, Tailor, &c. 5, St. Swithin's lane

Le Grice, Capt. 19, Surry street

Leman Abraham, Grocer and Tea Dealer, 14, London-lane

Lenham John, at the Waterman, 58, King-street

Lenny Isaac, Landsurveyor, 25, Tombland

Lens Mrs. 19, St. Giles'

Letree William, Esq. 13, St. Saviour's lane

Leverington Robert, Surveyor and Builder, 3, All Saint's Green

Life James, Shopkeeper, 26, King street

Lillestone Robert, Whitesmith, 56, Coslany-street

Lindley George, Nursery and Seeds Man, Catton

Ling Gouldsmith, Linen-Draper, 13, Market-place

Ling Arthur, Bricklayer, St. Stephen's Back street

Linstead Henry, Butcher, 46, Ber-street

Linstead Samuel, Butcher, 10, Fish-market

Litchfield George, Post-master, Post-Office, Market-place

Lock Nathaniel, Carpenter and Millwright, 41, Wymer street

Lock John, Accountant, 10, Red Well-street

Love Samuel, Plumber, &c. 115, Magdalen street

Love Robert Plumber &c. 53, Coslany street

Lovick John, Woollen-Draper, Button Seller and Haberdasher, 13, Cockey-lane

Lowden John, Butcher, 28, Market-place

Lowden James, Butcher, 36, ditto

Lowden John, jun. 6, Willow lane, St. Giles'

Lusher Thomas, Swan, 8, Swan-lane

Lubbock Richard, M. D. 76, St. Giles'

Lubbock Margaret, Baker, 24, Surry-street

Lubbock Thomas, Attorney, 25, Bethel-street

Lyons R. Optician, 1, Gun-lane

M

Mack William and Co. London Stage Waggons, 73, St. Giles' Broad street

Mack William, Collector of Freightage, &c. 29, St Giles'

Mack James, Pawnbroker, 45, Magdalen street

Mackie W. A. Nurseryman, St. Stephen's road

Maidwell James, Clock and Watch Maker, 8, Upper Westwick street

Mallet Nicholas, Shawl Manufacturer, 5, Muspole-street

Maltby Thomas, Merchant, 64, Gildengate street

Maltby Daniel, Shopkeeper, 63, Cowgate-street

Mann E. G. Appraiser and Auctioneer, 6, Dove-lane

Mann Robert, Clock and Watch Maker, 5, St. Simon's

Mann Samuel, Hair-Dresser, 20, Fye-bridge street

Mann Michael, Coppersmith and Brazier, 27, London-lane

Manning John, M. D. 20, Surry-street

Manning Edward, Coppersmith, Brazier, and Tin-plate Worker, 22, Cockey-lane

Manning John, Baker, 2, Coslany Bridge-street

Margetson Richard, Wheelwright, 16, St. Stephen's road

Marker Robert, Shopkeeper, 22, St. Augustine's street

Marley Susannah, Porter and Punch House, 29, Market-place

Marsh Edward, Merchant, 124, Magdalen street

Marsh Robert and Co. London Stage Waggons, 4, Tombland

Marsh James, Attorney, 3, Bank Place

Marshall Z. Ashley, and at the Angel, Norwich, on Saturdays

Marston Robert, Stone Mason, 48, Bethel street

Martlock James, 30, Recruiting Serjeant, Rampant Horse-street

Martin Sarah, Lamb Inn, Hay-market

Martin George Richard, Draper, Haberdasher, and Mercer, 17, Cockey-lane

Martin Edmund, Umbrella-Maker, and China-Man, 38, London-lane

Martin Samuel, Cabinet Maker, 2, Surry-street

Martin Charles, Upholder, 26, Hungate-street

Martin William, Hatter, &c. 2, Little Cockey-lane

Martineau Thomas, Esq. Magdalen-street

Martineau Philip, Surgeon, 192, King-street

Mason Robert, Esq. 70, Pottergate-street

Mason and Tidd, Druggists, &c. 7, Elm hill str.

Massey and Roberts, Shawl Manufacturers, 97, Pottergate-str.

Masters Mrs. Glover, 4, Red Lion-lane

Matcalf William, Shawl Manufacturer, 20, Colegate-street

Matthews William, Importer of Wine and Foreign Spirits, at the Golden Key, 24, Hay-market

Matthews John, Plumber, &c. 5, St. Stephen's street

Mays William, Carpenter, &c. 35, Pottergate-street

Mead William, Green Lion, 36, Cowgate-street

Mear Stephen, Builder, &c. 24, St. Stephen's Back street

Meek James, Plumber, 15, Magdalen-street

Mendham Elizabeth, Milliner, 33, St. Giles'

Mendham Thomas, Gardner, 21, St. Martin's at Oak street

Merry Peter, Plumber &c. 31, Magdalen street

Merry Robert, Cooper, 115, Pottergate-street

Merriment Jonathan, Throwsterer, 13, Cowgate-street

Middleton Rev. 4, Life's Green

Middleton Michael, Broker, 10, Bridewell Alley

Mileham Richard, at the Barley Mow, 1, Weaver's lane

Mileham Peter, Porter Merchant, 42, Wymer-street

Miles Edward, Tailor, 50, Bethel-street

Miles Stephen, Whalebone Staithe, 118, King-street

Millard Rev. Charles, 41, Snailgate street

Millard Rev. Charles, 4, Bracondale hill

Miller Samuel, at the Lamb, 135, Ber-street

Miller James, Hair Dresser, 119, Magdalen-street

Mills William, Upholsterer, Monument Yard, London, and at the Swan, Norwich

Mingay and Co. Woollen Drapers and Mercers, 22, Rampant Horse street

Mingay Richard, Master of Bridewell

Minner John, Rainbow Inn, 132, King-street

Minns Robert, Boot and Shoe Maker, 3, Back of the Inns

Mitchell Robert, at the Cock, 53, St. Giles'

Mitchell Samuel, Red Lion, 3, Coslany street

Mollet Rising, Whitesmith, Pig-lane

Monday Mrs. Broker, 28, Rampant Horse street

Moore John, Wheelwright, 18, Ber-street

Moore Thomas, Hawker and Pedlar's Office, 47, Bethel str.

Moore Theodore, Throwsterer, 150, King-street

Moore Stephen, Gent. 4, Lower Close

Moore James and Son, Dyers, 7, Wymer-street

Moore John, Sack Manufacturer, 30, Magdalen-street

Morley Charles, Stover and Throwsterer, 52, Cowgate-street

Morris John, Whitesmith, Appraiser and Auctioneer, at the Black Boys, 44, Colegate street

Morphew John, Attorney, 2, Wilkes's lane, near Bank-Place

Moss John, Esq. 7, Upper Surry street, and Porter Brewery, 57, St. Martin's at Oak street

Moss Richard, Gent. 19, Upper Close

Moltin Francis, Weather Glass Maker, 11, Lower Westwick street

Mountain Henry, Corn and Coal Merchant, 23, Lower Close

Mountney Thomas, Swan Inn, Upper Market str.

Munney John, Broker, 37, St. Giles'

Murray Mrs. 130, Magdalen street

Murry J. M. Appraiser and Auctioneer, 10, Black Horse Inn, St. Giles' Broad street

Muskett Thomas, Gressenhall, Tanner

Muskett Joseph, Easton Hall, and at the Swan, Upper Market str. Norwich, on Saturdays

N

Nash John, Importer and Dealer in Wines, &c. 33, Wymer-street

Neale James, Straw-Hat Manufacturer, 15, Bethel street

Neech Samuel, at the Public Gardens, St. Stephen's road

Neel Edward, Pastry Cook, &c. 21, Back of the Inns

Neeve William, Bricklayer, 143, Ber-street, late Scole's Green

Negus Mrs. 19, Lower Close

Nelson Charles, Landsurveyor, 7, Red Lion-lane

Newbegin Ann, Clothes' Broker, 1, Madder-market-street

Newman Richard, Baker, 126, Magdalen-street

Newson William, Grocer and Tea-Dealer, 101, Stump Cross

Newstead Samuel, Ladies' Shoe Maker, 17, Madder-market-street

Newstead John, at the Cat and Fiddle, 48, Magdalen-street

Newton Francis, Gent. 10, St. Stephen's street

Newton Rev. I. W. 16, Lower Close

Nicholas Robert, Hempen Cloth Manufacturer, Beccles, and in Weaver's lane, on Saturdays

Nichols Thomas, Rope Maker, 8, St. Augustine's street

Nickless Isaac, Raven Inn, 32, King-street

Nockles Samuel, Boot and Shoe Maker, 8, Elm hill street

Norgate Elias, Gent. 17, St. Giles'

Norgate and Stafford, Hair-Dressers, 18, Rampant Horse-str.

Norgate John, Grocer and Tea Dealer, 36, Surry-street

Norgate Mary, Glover, &c. 17, Dove-lane

Norman Benjamin, Hempen-Cloth Manufacturer, 4, Hog-hill

Norman James, Smith, 83, Ber-street

Norman John, Duke of York, Castle Ditches

Norman Thomas, at the Pine Apple, Trowse

Norris Jeremiah, Esq. 2, St. Giles' hill-street

Norris Samuel, Coffin Maker, 133, Magdalen street

Nosworthy James, Jeweller and Toyman, 3, Queen-street

Nudd John, Esq. Bracondale hill

Nunn Sarah, Baker, 10, St. Andrew's Chancery street

Nutter Sarah, Gingerbread Baker, 15, Cockey-lane

O

Oaker Joseph, Gent. 6, Snailgate-street

Oakley William, Smith, 3, St. Martin's by Palace street

Oliver Thomas, Gent. 11, Snailgate-street

Ollett George, Sun and Anchor Tavern, 51, Colegate street

Orsborn Mark, Tallow Chandler, 33, Timberhill-street

Orsborn Robert, Sandland's Ferry

Orsburn Edward, Livery Stables, Gildengate-street

Osborn and Son, Boot and Shoe Makers, 3, Upper Market str.

Osborn James and Co. Sack Manufacturers, 31, Cowgate street

Ownsworth John, Bricklayer, 27, Bethel-street

Oxley John, Hatter and Hosier, 5, Market-place; Dwelling-house, 4, Gildengate-street

Oxley Joseph, Merchant, 52, Gildengate-street

P

Page and Co. Grocers, 1, Timberhill-street

Page John, Baker, Jack of Newberry yard, Pottergate street

Page William, Accomptant, 22, St. Martin's at Oak street

Page James Cocksedge, 145, Ber-street

Pairman Jeremiah, Horse Dealer, 4, Orford-street

Painter Henry, Broker, 4, Upper Westwick street

Palmer William, Corn Merchant, 54, King-street

Palmer William, Grocer, &c. 63, Coslany street

Palmer William, Boot and Shoe Maker, 13, Fyebridge street

Parkinson Joseph, Haberdasher, 37, London-lane

Parkerson I. C. Corn and Coal Merchant, 18, St. Martin's by Palace street

Parkerson John, House-Bell Hanger and Venetian Blind-Maker, 9, Hungate-street

Parke Luke, Carver and Gilder, 9, Little Cockey-lane

Parlour John, Whitesmith, 15, London-lane

Parmerton John, Miller, Aylsham, and at the Angel, Norwich

Parr Rev. Robert, 67, St. Giles' Broad street

Parr Thomas, Woollen Draper, 5, Pottergate-street

Parslee Mrs. Bell Inn, 17, Hog hill

Partridge Robert, Esq. 3, Gildengate street

Partridge Rev. Mr. 10, Lower Goat-lane

Paston Mrs. 4, Lady's lane

Pastons James, Grocer and Tallow Chandler, 116, Ber-street

Patteson John, Esq. 6, Surry street

Pater John, Carpenter, 2, Golden Dog-lane

Paul William, Appraiser, Auctioneer, and House-Broker, 98, Upper Westwick-street

Payne John, Printer, Bookseller, and Stationer, 22, Market-place

Peck William, Innkeeper, 30, Market-place

Peck James, Turk's Head, 4, Weaver's lane

Peck Edward, Butcher, 1, Fish-market

Peck Mary, Butcher, 50, Ber-street

Peele Rev. John, 5, Lady's lane

Perkins William, Tin-plate Worker, 11, Little Cockey-lane

Perkins William, Coppersmith, 25, Hay-market

Perown James, Boulting Cloth Maker, 15, Coslany-street

Perry Paul, Turner, 13, St. Gregory's Church yard

Peete Richard, Esq. 22, Surry-street

Phillips William, Peacock, 78, St. Stephen's street

Phillips John, Griffin Inn, 1, King-street

Pickis Robert, Oatmeal Maker, 6, Castle Ditches

Pigg Joseph, Carpenter and Joiner, Fishgate-street

Pigg Robert, Confectioner, &c. 28, London-lane

Pigg Thomas and Joseph, Carpenters and Joiners, 16, St. Saviour's lane

Pillans W. C. Esq. 3, Tomland

Pitchford, Surgeon, 26, St. Giles' Broad street

Pitcher Isaiah, Pawn Broker, 26, Pottergate-street

Pitchers James, Hair Dresser, 10, Upper Market str.

Plaford John, China and Glass Warehouse, 38, Market-place

Platter James, Boot and Shoe Maker, 9, Tooley-street

Playford Robert, Patten and Trunk Maker, 4, Dove-lane

Plumber and Massey, Ironmongers, &c. 124, Pottergate-street

Plumbtree Robert, Esq. 84, Ber-street

Pooley Thomas, Duffield and Rug Maker, 71, Magdalen-street

Pooley Sarah, Duffield Manufacturer, Bird and Hand lane, Heigham

Pope Richard, Carpenter, 86, Upper Westwick-street

Potter Rev. 7, Upper Close

Potter William, Currier, 33, Lower Westwick-street

Potter Charles, Accomptant, St. Martin's at Oak street

Powell Robert, Woolcomber, 114, Magdalen street

Prentice Samuel, Shakspeare Tavern, 24, London-lane

Prentice Susannah, Wine Vaults, 34, London-lane

Prentice Robert, Importer and Dealer in Wines, &c. 11, Tombland

Prest Robert, Baker, 14, Pitt-street

Preston Elizabeth, White Lion Inn, White Lion-lane

Priest Robert, Grocer and Tea Dealer, 42, Market-place

Priest John Fox, Chymist and Druggist, 1, St. Giles' Broad str.

Prior William, Horse and Groom, 17, Back of the Inns

Pritchard Jonathan, Baker, 20, Fish-gate street

Pritchard John, Baker, 15, St. George's Bridge-street

Procter Joseph, D. D. 14, Upper Close

Purland Robert, Chymist, &c. 3, Fyebridge-street

Purland Robert, sen. Surgeon, in Court, 32, Cowgate-street

Purland Matthew, at Whittington and his Cat, 20, Cowgate street

Purnell John, Throwsterer, 12, Cowgate-street

Pye Samuel, Attorney, 22, St. Martin's by Palace plain

Pye Richard, Tailor, 2, St. Gregory's Church-yard

Q

Quantrell Robert, Baker, 45, Coslany-street

R

Rackham Matthew, Intwood Hall, and at the Swan, Upper Market str. on Saturdays

Rackham Elizabeth, Grocer, 34, St. Stephen's street

Rackham John, Baker, 39, St. Stephen's street

Rackham Matthew, Bull Inn, 43, ditto

Rackham Mrs. Baker, 6, Upper Goat-lane

Rackham Rebecca, Shopkeeper, 1, Peacock street

Rackham William, Leather Cutter, 71, Coslany-street

Ramm William, Gent. 187, King-street

Rampley George, Crown Inn, 32, Upper Westwick-street

Rand Hewett, Esq. Sampson and Hercules' Court, Tombland

Rand William Fell, Surgeon, ditto, ditto

Randall Benjamin, Esq. 16, Upper Close

Ransome Thomas, Gent. 14, Castle Meadow

Raymes Thomas, Oatmeal Maker, 18, St. Simon's

Reeves James, China and Glass Warehouse, 23, Cockey-lane

Reeve Isaac, Duffield and Flushing Manufacturer, 1, Golden Dog lane

Reeve Thomas and Co. Clothiers, 7, Soutergate-street

Reeve John Sayer, Baker, 18 and 19, ditto

Reynolds John, Iron Merchant, 12, Lower Goat-lane

Reynolds Charles, Woollen Draper, 19, Market-place

Reuben William, Cooper, 13, Ber-street

Rice Luke, Tailor, 3, Rampant Horse-street

Richer Nicholas, Bookbinder, 6, St. Giles' Broad street

Riches William, George Inn, 37, St. Stephen's street

Riches Thomas, Hair Preparer, &c. 4, Wastlegate str. All Saints

Riches Edward, Hair Dresser, 10, Pottergate-street

Riches Henry, Granaries and Coal Binns, late Burrell's, 120, King-street

Riches John, Carpenter, Soutergate-street

Richards Edward, Licensed to Let Post Horses, &c. &c. 32, Botolph-street

Richards Robert, Linen Manufacturer, 26, Market-place

Rider Robert, Billiard-Table Maker, 1, King-street

Rigby Edward, Esq. Surgeon, 64, St. Giles' Broad street

Riggs John, Prince of Wales, 2, Back of the Inns

Riggs John, Brewer's Arms, 18, London-lane

Ringer Edward, Boot and Shoe Maker, 14, Dove-lane

Rippon James, Tailor, &c. 3, Surry-street

Riseborough John, Coal Merchant, 9, Chapel-field-lane

Rivett S. Silk Dyer, 17, Upper Market

Rix R. and Co. Glass Warehouse, 47, Wymer-street N.B. Agent to the Sun Fire-Office

Roach Richard, Plumber, &c. 3, St. Simon's

Roach Edward, Tailor, 129, Magdalen-street

Roberts John, Glover, &c., 17, Golden Ball-lane

Roberts John Whitaker, Hotpresser, 12, Soutergate-street

Robinson James, Surgeon, 16, Lower Goat-lane

Robinson John, Plumber, &c. 9, Snailgate-street

Robinson William, Hotpresser, 15, ditto

Robinson Charles, Lock and White Smith, 21, St. Martin's at Oak lane

Rodwell John, Dyer, 42, Lower Westwick-street

Roe Robert, Boot and Shoe Maker, 14, Cockey-lane

Roe Bosom, Baker, 7, Fyebridge-street

Roe John, Tailor, &c. 5, Swan-lane

Rogers Mrs. Ladies' Boarding School, Magdalen-street

Rooks John, Deal, Timber Merchant, and Builder, 12, Fishgate-street

Root James, Whitesmith, 4, St. Saviour's Church lane

Roope James, Cabinet-Maker, 6, Timberhill-street

Rose Thomas, Cork Cutter, 69, St. Stephen's street

Rose Mary, Silk Dyer, 3, Swan-lane

Royal Peter, at the Chequers, 67, Coslany-street

Royal Benjamin, Millwright, 18, Tooley-street

Rowe James, Two Quarts, 17, St Stephen's street

Rudd Robert, Baker, Rising Sun-lane

Rudd John, Shopkeeper, 34, Botolph-street

Rudd John, Shopkeeper, 36, Gildengate street

Russells Mary, Broker, 5, Hog-hill

Rump and Clipperton, Grocers, Tea Dealers and Hop Factors, 13, Hay-market

Rump James, jun. Gent. Catton

Russell Skinner, Attorney, 1, in Court, opposite the Black Horse, St. Giles'

Russell Jeremiah, Tripeman, 136, Ber-street

Russell Edward, Clock and Watch Maker, 25, Magdalen-street

Rust Edward, Haberdasher, 19, Tombland

Rye William, Linen-Draper, 18, Upper Market

S

Sabbarton James and Co. Woolcombers, 32, Pitt-street

Sadd John, Dyer, 65, Coslany-street

Salmon Richard, Tailor, 3, St. Saviour's Church-lane

Salmon Thomas, Baker, 52, Ber-street

Salmon Thomas, Baker, 102, Magdalen-street

Sampson Aaron, Confectioner, 11, Lower Goat-lane

Sandby Rev. Paul, D. D. Chancellor, 1, Lower Close square

Saul William, Carpenter, &c. 4, St. Giles' hill

Say Thomas, Plumber, &c. 14, St. Giles'

Say Thomas, Plumber, &c. St. Martin's by Palace street

Sawter Peter, Collar-maker, Trowse

Schuldham John, Woollen-Draper and Mercer, 8, Market place

Scott Daniel, Esq. 125, Magdalen-street

Scott Peter, Brush Maker, 19, White Lion-lane

Scott John, Upholder, 15, White Lion-lane

Scott James, Baker, 24, St. Stephen's street

Scott Thomas, Woollen Manufacturer, 29, Fishgate-street

Scott Robert, Surgeon, 39, ditto

Scott William, Flower in Hand, 15, Tooley-street

Seggins Isaac, King's Head Inn, 38, St. Giles'

Sewell Joseph, Attorney, 2, Fromanteel's Court, Chapel-Field-lane

Sewell Robert, Calico Glazier, 4, in Court, opposite the Black Horse, St. Giles'

Sewell Bartholomew, Merchant, 35, Pitt-street

Sewell John, Bracon Ash, and at the Rampant Horse, St. Stephen's, on Saturdays

Sexton Joseph, Shawl Manufacturer, 46, Snailgate-street

Sexton William, Ironmonger, 49, Market-place

Shalders Absalom, Sadler, &c. 8, Upper Market str.

Shalders William, Leather Cutter, 14, Fyebridge-street

Shalders Jacob, Grocer, 3, St. George's Bridge-street

Sharpe Robert, Tailor and Habit Maker, 29, Rampant Horse street

Sherrell Mary, Milliner, 11, Cockey-lane

Shepard James, House Broker, 17, Rampant Horse street

Shelty Thomas, Gent. 7, Snailgate-street

Shickle James, Plasterer, 22, Hungate-street

Shildrake John, Tailor and Habit Maker, 43, Lower Westwick-street

Shildrake Thomas, Hampshire Hog, 63, Lower Westwick-street

Shreeve Ann, Shopkeeper, 30, St. Augustine's street

Shreeve and Newton, Silversmiths and Haberdashers, 20, Cockey-lane

Sidel John, Boot and Shoe Maker, 13, Magdalen street

Sidney John, Gardner, Snailgate-street

Siely and Wright, Linen-Drapers, 36, London-lane

Siely Thomas, Furrier, 3, Upper Westwick-street

Sillet William, at the Duke of York, Cow-hill

Sillis Francis, Farmer, Lime Burner, and Brick Maker, Lakenham, and at the King's Head, Norwich, on Saturdays. Brick Kiln, near Brazen Doors

Silvey Robert, Gingerbread Baker, 21, Bethel-street

Sizeland Thomas, Baker, 43, Bethel-street

Sims John, Chymist and Druggist, 26, London-lane

Simpson William, Attorney, 24, St. Giles'

Simpson Robert, 79, Curriers' Arms, St. Giles'

Skelton Thomas, Broker, 8, Madder-market-street

Skeele Henry, at the Coffee House, late Tuck's, 4, Market-place

Slater John, Farrier, 16, Hay-market

Sly and Son, Clock and Watch Makers 1, White Lion-lane, and 61, Gildengate-street

Smith Francis, Cooper, 76, St. Stephen's street

Smith Thomas, Engraver, 11, Bethel-street

Smith William, Esq. 6, Lady's lane

Smith Jacob, Baker, 1, Common Pump street

Smith John, Carpenter, 146, Ber street

Smith William, James, and Francis, Woollen-Drapers, 6, Market-place

Smith Thomas, Furrier and Liquor Merchant, 43, Market-place

Smith William, Plumber, &c. 7, Upper Market

Smith James, Ladies' Shoe Maker, 9, ditto

Smith Daniel, Fishmonger, 17, Fish-market

Smith Thomas, Cabinet Maker, 16, St. Giles'

Smith Samuel, Grocer, 42, ditto

Smith William, Tanner, 2, in Court opposite the Black Horse, St. Giles'. Tanning Office at Thorpe

Smith Eli, Duffield Maker, 25, St Stephen's street

Smith Thomas, Tailor and Habit Maker, 16, Hungate-street

Smith James, Attorney, in Goss's yard, Elm hill-street

Smith John, Hempen-Cloth Manufacturer, 18, Wymer-str.

Smith James, Grocer, 20, Coslany-street

Smith Moses, Pawn Broker, 50, St. Martin's at Oak-street

Smith Hugh, Gardner and Seedsman, without Brazen Doors

Smith Matthew, Tanner, 7, Heigham-street

Snell I. C. M.D. 172, King-street,

Sothern George, Chymist, &c. 25, Market-place

Sothern Jane, Glass Warehouse, 10, Swan-lane

Southgate John, Plumber, 8, Timberhill-street

Spalding Daniel, Grocer and Liquor Merchant, 4, Elm hill str.

Sparkes Robert, at the Hole in the Wall 43, Wymer-street

Sparkles Edward, Duke of York, 11, Barrack street

Sparks Britton, Licensed to Let Post Horses, &c. 23, Elm hill

Sparshall Edmund, Wine, Rum, Brandy and Hop Merchant, Dealer in Burton Ale, London Porter, Herefordshire Cyder and Perry, 132, Magdalen-street, Corner of St. Clement's Church-yard

Spencer John, New Common Staithe, 123, King-street

Spinks John, Woolpack, 17, Muspole-street

Spooner Thomas, Boot and Shoe Maker, 31, Market-place

Spooner Thomas, Boot and Shoe Maker, 7, Castle Ditches

Spratts Messrs. Coach, Harness and Wheel Manufacturers, 6, Chapel-field

Spratt James, Pawnbroker, 16, Golden Ball-lane

Spratt John, Pawnbroker, 6, Upper Westwick-street

Springall Thomas, Wheat Sheaf, 3, Bethel-street

Springfield Daniel, at the Yarmouth Bridge, 16, Red Lion-lane

Springfield Ann, Moon and Stars, 29, Colegate-street

Springfield Edmund, Pawnbroker, 1, St George's Church Alley

Spurrell Robert, Grocer, 65, Ber-street

Squire Edward, Corn Merchant, 141, Old Common Staithe, King-street

Squire Edward, Merchant, Dwelling House, 1, Tombland

Stacey George, Chymist, &c. 12, White Lion-lane

Staff John, Grocer and Tallow Chandler, 5, St. Martin's by Palace-street

Staff John, Baker, 152, King street

Stafford Robert, Shopkeeper, 46, Coslany-street

Stag James, Nurseryman, at Yarmouth, and at Murry's, Black Horse, St Giles'

Stannard William, Master of St. Andrew's Workhouse

Stannard Joseph, Carpenter, 12, Upper Westwick-street

Stannard John, Plumber, &c. 61, ditto

Stannard James, City Engineer, 11, Rose-lane

Stannard Richard, Hosier and Mercer, 14, Market-place

Stannard Joseph and Son, House Builders, 10, Colegate-street

Starling Thomas, Boot and Shoe Maker, 49, Botolph-street

Starling John Parlett, Coal Merchant, Life's Green

Starry George, Whitesmith, 3, Fishgate-street

Stebbing Henry, Stay Maker, 64, St. Stephen's street

Stebbing Robert, Sadler, 3, Little Rampant Horse street

Stevenson and Matchett, Printers and Stationers, 47, Market-place

Stevenson William, Esq. Dwelling House, 34, Surry-street

Stevenson William, Farrier, 1, Castle Meadow

Stevens William, Grocer and Tallow Chandler, 13, Madder-market, and Cabinet and Chair Maker, 14

Steward Robert, Baker, 27, Colegate-street

Steward Charles, Throwsterer, 4, Coslany-street

Stewart Jane and Ann, Haberdashers, 35, London-lane

Steward William, Baker, 39, London-lane

Steward John, Attorney, Upper Heigham, and Agent to the Phœnix Fire Office, Surry-street

Stewart James, Importer and Dealer in Foreign Spirits, &c. 13, Lower Close

Stimpson Samuel, Crown Inn, 12, St. Stephen's street

Stoddart John, Coach Maker, St. Giles' road

Stone William, Boot and Shoe Maker, 7, Bridewell Alley

Stone Francis, Surveyor and Builder, 135, King-street

Storey J. B. Wharfinger, Music-House Staithe, 139, King-street

Storey John, Farmer, Wymondham, and at the George, St. Stephen's, on Saturdays

Storey John, Woolcomber, 23, Coslany-street

Stoughton Thomas, Attorney, 5, King-street

Strange James, Coach-Maker, 34, Timberhill-street

Studwell Elizabeth, Glass and China Warehouse, 35, Market-place

Sturgeon Mrs. 3, Lower Close

Sudbury James and Son, Upholders, 5, Cockey-lane

Sudbury Samuel, Gent. 7, All Saints' Green

Suffield R. and G. Wine and Liquor Merchants, 45, St. Giles'

Sunstead Daniel, Grocer, 10, Soutergate-street

Sutton Rev. Charles, 197, King-street

Swan William, Tinman and Brazier, 121, Magdalen-street

Swaine and Wright, Plasterers, 18, Gildengate-street

Sword Benjamin, Licensed to Let Post Horses, Chaises, &c. 6, King street

Syder John, Hop Merchant, Importer and Dealer in Foreign Spirits, Wymondham, and at the Wounded Heart, Upper Market, Norwich, on Saturdays

Syder Haylett, Hosier, &c. Wymondham, and at Mrs. Studwell's, Market place, Norwich, on Saturdays

Syer Thomas, at the Dove, 13, Lower Westwick-street

Syer John, Staymaker, 9, Red-Well-street

Symonds William, Master Weaver, 8, St. Andrew's Bridge str.

T

Tallack John, 1, Duke's Palace

Tawell Thomas, Esq. Iron Merchant, 22, Upper Close. N.B. The Iron Warehouse, 7, Wastlegate-lane, All Saints

Taylor Rev. Thomas, 34, Bethel street

Taylor Adam, Attorney, 21, Hog-hill

Taylor Charles, Upholder, 44, London-lane

Taylor Charles, Dwelling house, 20, Castle Meadow

Taylor Matthew, House Steward, 70, King-street

Taylor Thomas, Upholder, 4, Pottergate-street

Taylor John, Plumber and Glazier, 6, St. Martin's by Palace street

Taylor Richard, Wool Factor, 72, Upper Westwick-street

Taylor and Barnard, Wool Factors, 12, Muspole-street

Taylor Adam, Swardeston, and at the Angel, Norwich, on Saturdays

Theobald John, Breeches Maker, 21, Cockey-lane

Theobald William, Breeches Maker, &c. 16, White Lion-lane

Theobald S. and A. Milliners, 4, St. George's Bridge street

Thirtle John, Boot and Shoe Maker, 106, Magdalen-street

Thompson William, Boot and Shoe Maker, 28, St. Giles'

Thompson Peter, Gate-House Inn, Upper Close

Thompson John, Shopkeeper, White Friars' Bridge street

Thompson John, Shopkeeper, 1, Cowgate-street

Thompson John, Gent. 16, St. Augustine's street

Thompson John, Porter Merchant, 39, Colegate-street

Thorsby John, Baker, 39, Lower Westwick-street

Thurgar Charles, Ladies' Boarding School, in Court, Queen's street

Thurlow Henry, Rope Maker, 39, St Martin's at Oak-street

Thurlow Rev. E. S. 31, Lower Close

Thurston John, Broker, 12, Wymer-street

Thurston Samuel, Broker, 15, ditto

Thwaites Alexander, Linen Draper, and Hempen Cloth Manufacturer, 22, London-lane

Tillett William, Confectioner, 18, St. Stephen's street

Tillet James, Whitesmith, 112, Pottergate-street

Tillett Samuel, Patten Maker, 10, Little Cockey-lane

Tillyard Robert, Manufacturer, 21, Fishgate-street

Tilgat Susannah, Butcher, Fish-market

Tinkler John, Currier, 41, Lower Westwick-street

Tinkler John, jun. and Co. Tanners, 15, Heigham-street

Tipple Thomas, Tailor, &c. 19, Tooley-street

Todd Samuel, Patten Maker, 30, Timberhill-street

Toll John and Co. Woollen and Linen Drapers, 17, Market-place

Toll John, jun. Hatter and Hosier, 23, Market-place

Toll George, Glass and China Warehouse, 12, Hay-market

Toll John, Dwelling House, 11, St. Faith's lane

Tomlinson Robert, Stay maker, 4, Chancery street, St. Andrew's

Tomlinson William, Hatter and Hosier, 11, Back of the Inns

Tompson Thomas, Broker and Salesman, 8, White Lion-lane

Tompson Timothy, Common Beer Brewer, 37, King-street

Tompson Thomas and Son, Merchants, 98, ditto

Tompson Rev. John, 7, Bank Place

Town Daniel, Licensed to Let Post Horses, 11, Upper Goat-lane

Trafford Sigismund, Esq. Tuck's Wood, Lakenham

Treasure William, Rope Maker, 66, Magdalen-street

Trigg Francis, Tailor, 8, Bethel-street

Troughton Thomas, Woolcomber, 8, Colegate-street

Tubby Samuel, Cabinet Maker, 77, St. Stephen's street

Turner Joseph, D.D. Dean of Norwich

Turner Thomas, Engraver and Jeweller, 17, London-lane

Turner Nicholas, Linen Manufacturer, 8, St. Gregory's Church-yard

Turner John, Carpenter, &c. 111, Pottergate-street

Turner Thomas, Carpenter, &c. 44, Cowgate-street

Turner Robert, Housebroker, 16, Soutergate-street

Tuthill Charles, Merchant, 38 and 39, Pitt-street

Tuthill John, Esq. 3, Willow-lane, St Giles'

V

Varnish Elizabeth, Butcher, 48, Ber-street

Varnish Edward, Butcher, 34, Market-place

Varnish Benjamin, Butcher, 51, Ber-street

Vincent Edward, Boot and Shoe Maker, 22, Back of the Inns

Vincent William, Boot and Shoe Maker, 9, Lower Westwick street

U

Upcroft William, Shopkeeper, 18, Magdalen-street

Upcroft John, Sawyer's Arms, 37, Upper Westwick-street

Utton William, Attorney, 6, Tombland

W

Wade John, Shopkeeper, 24, All Saints' Green

Wade James, Butcher, 24, Upper Market

Wade Christopher, Butcher, 25, Upper Market

Wagstaff John, Miller and Baker, 21, Coslany-street

Waites Elizabeth, Broker, 2, Lower Westwick-street

Waite George, Tailor, 23, London-lane

Waite John, White Hart, 10, Coslany-street

Wall Marke, Hempen-Cloth Manufacturer, 3, Weaver's lane

Wake Henry, Angel Inn, 16, Market-place—N.B. Since this work was begun, Mr. John Ball has taken it.

Walker Isaac, Gunsmith, 5, Briggs'-lane

Walker Benjamin, Gent. 2, Goodman's yard, St. Stephen's

Walker Rev. John, 24, Lower Close

Walker John, Bricklayer, Lower Westwick-street

Walker Amies, Baker, 70, Coslany-street

Walkington James, Lace Manufacturer, 75, St. Giles'

Walpole William, Bricklayer, 13, Colegate-street

Ward Robert, Butcher, 11, Fish market

Ward Robert, Sadler and Ironmonger, 8, Briggs' lane; and 9, Rampant-Horse-street. Dwelling-house, 19, Castle Meadow

Ward John, Baker, 1, Red Lion-lane

Ward Thomas, Baker, St. Stephen's road

Ward William, Butcher, 109, Ber-street

Ward John, Patten Maker, 34, Upper Westwick-street

Warden John, Hot-presser, 18, Peacock street

Wardlaw Mrs. Bookseller, 16, Dove-lane

Warne John, Hair-Dresser, 13, Queen-street

Warne George, Musician, 1, Cook's lane, King-street

Warne L. Clearstarcher, 7, Colegate-street

Warne Benjamin, Staymaker, Gilden Craft lane

Warner William, Smith, 29, St. Stephen's street

Waters George, Lion and Castle, 11, Timberhill-street

Watering Stephen, Elephant Inn, 108, Magdalen street, N.B. Now kept by Charles Browne, late of the Lion and Castle Inn, Jail hill

Watling James, Tailor, 51, St. Giles'

Watson John, Baker, 11, White Lion-lane

Watson Edward, Coal Merchant, 2, St. Ann's Staithe, King-street

Watson John, Tailor, Jack of Newberry yard, Pottergate-street

Watson Richard, Farrier, 109, Pottergate-street

Watson Joseph, Tailor, 2, Maddermarket-street

Watson Thomas, Esq. Merchant, 5, Coslany-street

Watts James, Butcher, 45, Ber-street

Watts Mary, Butcher, 1, Hall's End

Wayte Thomas, Oatmeal Maker, 6, Wastlegate-lane, All Saints

Weaver William, Shopkeeper, 130, Ber-street

Webster William, Maid's Head Inn, 1, Fyebridge-street

Webster Rev. Stephen, Ber-street road

Webster James, Boot and Shoe Maker, Cross-lane, St. George's

Weeks William, Plumber, 20, Botolph-street

Wells Mary, Pawnbroker, 3, St. Martin's at Oak street

Wells William, Attorney, 1, Theatre square

Wells John, Gent, 2, Queen-street

Wells Rev. John, 4, Upper Close

Weston Charles, Esq. and Co. Bankers, 15, Upper Market

Weston Charles, jun. Esq. Dwelling-House, 12, Queen-street

West John, Linen Draper, 3, Cockey-lane

Wetherley, Whitesmith, All Saints' Green

Whall Henry, Coach Master, 16, Muspole-street

Wharne Sarah, Shopkeeper, 2, St. Martin's by Palace street

Wheeler Mrs. 62, St. Giles'

When James, Gingerbread Baker, 6, St. Stephen's road

Whitaker Mrs. 33, Colegate-street

Whitbrook William, Brazier, 22, Wastlegate-street, All Saints

White Ann, Printer, 11, St. Andrew's Bridge street

White William, Gent. Thorpe

White William, at the Man Laden with Mischief, 20, St. Saviour's lane

Whittingham Rev. 3, Life's Green

Wickes Rice, Farmer, Eaton, and at the Greyhound, St. Stephen's, on Wednesdays and Saturdays

Wiffen Abraham, Boot and Shoe Maker, 72, St. Stephen's street

Wilcocks William, Merchant, 63 and 64, Pottergate-street

Wild William, Shopkeeper, 14, Barrack street

Wiley Thomas, Woolcomber, White Friars' Bridge street, now No. 2, Privy-lane

Willement Martin, Merchant, 1, Snailgate-street

Wilkins John, Dwelling-House, 11, St. Martin's at Oak lane

Wilkins James, Plasterer, St. Benedict's Church-yard

Wilkin Charles, Lion Cutter, 55, St. Stephen's street

Wilmot Robert, Hat Maker, 7, Dove-lane

Willmot Joseph, Hosier, 95, Upper Westwick-street

Wilsea Samuel, Cabinet-Maker, &c. 10 and 11, Madder-market-street

Willsea Peter, Plumber, 47, Coslany-street

Wilson Thomas, Baker and Pastry Cook, 18, Tombland

Wilson William, Boot and Shoe Maker, 114, Pottergate-str.

Wilson William, Calico Glazier, 4, Goodman's Yard, St. Stephen's street

Wimpres Hannah, Shopkeeper, 9, Bridewell Alley

Windett James, Grocer, 5, London lane

Winter James, Baker, 29, Wymer-street

Wilch John, Baker, 17, St. Martin's by Palace plain

Witham James, Music and Drawing Master, and Musical Instrument Seller, 7, London-lane

Witherick Jeremiah, at the Fountain, Briggs' lane

Woods James, Watch Maker, 2, Upper Market

Wood Hannah, Grocer and Tea Dealer, 74, St. Stephen's street, and 1, Surry-street

Woodbine John, Manufacturer, 13 and 14, Soutergate-street

Woodcock John, Hair Dresser, 8, Upper Market

Woodgate Philip, Woolcomber, 86, Magdalen-street

Woodhouse Elizabeth, Shoe Maker, 18, Back of the Inns

Woodhouse Rev. P. 11, Upper Close

Woodrow John, Gent. 4, Snailgate-street

Woods William, Licensed to Let Post Horses, &c. 8, Wilkes's lane, near Bank place

Woods John, Fishmonger, 18, Fish-market

Woods John, Cooper, 35, Coslany-street

Woods Thomas, Fearnought Maker, 64, ditto

Woodward John, Eating-House, 36, St. Stephen's-street

Woolford Joseph, Grocer and Tea Dealer, 47, London-lane

Woolston Mrs. at the Guild-hall Inn, 21, Upper Market

Woolverton William, School-master, 6, Elm hill str.

Worth and Co. Merchants, 14, Gildengate-street

Worth Walter, Dwelling house, 13, ditto

Wright Richard, Hempen Cloth Manufacturer, 2, Post-Office Court

Wright Robert, Grocer, &c. 8, King-street

Wright James, Gunsmith, 6, Queen-street

Wright John, Plasterer, late of Snailgate-street, now No. 75, Upper Westwick-street

Wright Robert, Bear and Staff, 14, Fisher's lane

Wright John, Coal Merchant, 36, Botolph-street

Wright Edward, Throwster, 6, Coslany-street

Wright Henry John, Plasterer, 37, Snailgate-street

Wright Cotton, Woolcomber, 8, St. Mary's Church yard

Wyatt Noah, Boot and Shoe Maker, 2, St. Stephen's street

Wymer George, Attorney, 40, Pottergate-street

Y

Yallop Daniel, at the Dolphin, 26, Coslany street

Yallop James, Unicorn, 42, ditto

Youngs Peter (at the City of Norwich), 5, Wastlegate, All Saints

Youngman Hannah, Tailor, 2, Little Rampant Horse-street

Youngman William, Scarlet Dyer, 33, Pitt street

Merchants, &c. attending at Inns in and near the Market-place, on Market-days.

Bloom D. and Co. 2, Duke's Palace, and Trowse Mills

Buck Robert, Florden, at the Rampant Horse, St. Stephen's

Buck John, St. Clement's Hill, and at the King's Head

Candler Lawrence and Son, Cringleford, and at the Rampant Horse, St. Stephen's

Carter J. G. Wyndham, and at the Coach-maker's Arms, St. Stephen's road

Barton William, Corn and Coal Merchant, 164, King-street

Marshall Z. Ashby, at the Angel

Parmeter John, Aylsham, and at the Angel

Sewell John, Bracon Ash, and at the Rampant Horse, St. Stephen's

Sillis Francis, Farmer, Lime-burner, and Brick-maker, Lakenham, and at the King's Head

Syder John, Hop-merchant, Importer, and Dealer in Foreign Spirits, Wyndham, and at the Wounded Heart, Upper-market

Foster Peter, Lenwade Mills, White Heart, St. Peter's

Dowson B. U. Geldestone, Blue Bell, Hog hill

Roper Thomas, Marlingford, White Swan, St. Peter's

Ames and Parkinson, Hellesdon Mills, at the King's Head, Market-place

Wright D. Saxlingham Mills, Rampant Horse

Candler and Son, Cringleford, Rampant Horse

Palgrave William and Thomas, Coltishall, Maid's Head, St. Simon's

Colls John, Horstead, King's Head, Magdalen-street

And several other Gentlemen who regularly attend at the Corn-Exchange, St. Andrews.

List of Bankers in Norwich.

Gurney Richard, Bartlett, and Joseph, 1, Bank-place

Harvey and Hudson, 198, King-street

Kerrison Sir Roger, Knt. and Co. 8, Back of the Inns

Kett and Back, 2, Hog-hill

Weston Charles, Esq. and Co. Bankers, 15, Upper-market

List of Surgeons.

Aldhouse Stephen, 2, Wymer-street

Back William, Wilkes's lane, near Bank-lane

Bokenham Thomas, 10, Upper Westwick-street

Bond William, 8, Tombland

Colman Edward, 12, Tombland

Chambers N. 5, Chapel-field

Dalrymple William, 40, Colegate-street

Donne, Eaton-road, without St. Giles

Keymer James, 5 Bethel-street

Martineau Philip, 192, King-street

Norgate Elias, 17, St. Giles'

Pitchford John, 26, St. Giles' Broad street

Purland Robert, sen. in Court, 32, Cowgate-street

Rand William Fell, Sampson and Hercules' Court, Tombland

Rigby Edward, Esq. 64, St. Giles' Broad street

Robinson James, 16, Lower Goat-lane

Scott Robert, 39, Fishgate-street

Physicians.

Alderson James, 3, Snailgate-street

Lubbock Richard, M.D. 76, St. Giles' Broad street

Manning John, 20, Surry-street

Beevor James, 72, St. Giles' Broad street

Beevor Henry, 58, ditto [42]

List of Attorneys at Law.

Amyott Thomas, 13, Upper Close

Atkinson John, 191, King-street

Barber Thomas, 2, St. Stephen's Back street

Blake Thomas, jun. Esq. 5, Queen-street

Boyce James, 11, Wymer-street

Chapman Gardiner, 9, Upper Close

De Hague Elisha, 5, Elm-hill-street

Foster, Son, Unthank, and Forster, 11, Queen-street

Bigg John, 40, Pottergate-street

Goodwin James, 2, Gun-lane

Ganning Daniel, Esq. 23, St. Giles'

Grand John, 37, Bethel-street

Harmer Henry, 6, Chapel-field-lane

Harmer Samuel, ditto

Hardy Charles, St. Michael's at Plea Church-Alley

Lay Charles, 40, St. Giles'

Lubbock Thomas, 25, Bethel-street

Marsh James, 3, Bank place

Morphew John, 2, Wilkes's lane, near Bank place

Pye Samuel, 22, St. Martin's by Palace plain

Russell Skinner, 1, in Court, opposite the Black Horse St. Giles'

Sewell Joseph, 2, Fromanteel's Court, Chapel-field-lane

Simpson William, 24, St. Giles'

Smith James, in Goss's Yard, Elm-hill-street

Stoughton Thomas, 5, King-street

Steward John, Upper-Heigham

Taylor Adam, 21, Hog-hill

Utton William, 6, Tombland

Wells William, 1, Theatre-square

Wymer George, 40, Pottergate-street

Woodcocke —, in Court, Hay hill

List of Boarding Schools for Young Ladies.

Coes (Miss), 1, Griffin-lane

Drakes (Miss), 31, All Saints' Green

Hickling (Miss), 8, Chancery-street, St. Andrew's

Hodgson James, 6, Wymer-street

Rogers (Mrs.), Magdalen-street

Thurgar Charles, in Court, Queen-street

Brands (Miss), Bethel-street

Browne (Miss), opposite St. Stephen's church

`Lodging and Boarding Houses.

Claxton John, St. Stephen's Church-yard

Pye (Mrs.) St. Gregory's

Wilson (Mrs.) Pottergate-street

List of Inns, &c.

Castle Inn, Mrs. Booth, 13, White Lion-lane

Black Horse Inn, 7, Tombland—John Burton

King's Head, 116, Magdalen-street—William Colls

White Hart Inn, St. Peter's—Elizabeth Cotton

White Horse Inn, 2, Hay-market—Robert Drake

White Lion, 44, Upper Westwick street

Rose Inn, 2, St. Augustine's—John Keymer

Star Inn, 9, Hay-market—John Larke

Waggon and Horses, 3, St. Giles' Broad-street—Wm. Laws

Waggon and Horses Inn, 13, Tombland—James Lea

KING'S HEAD INN, 11, Market-place—William Leach

Nag's Head Inn, 11, Rampant Horse street—Charles Leeds

Swan, 8, Swan-lane—Thomas Lusher

Lamb Inn, Haymarket—Sarah Martin

Swan Inn, Upper Market-street—Thomas Mountney

Raven Inn, 32, King-street—Isaac Nickless

Blue Bell Inn, 17, Hog-hill—Miss Parslee

Griffin Inn, 1, King-street—John Phillips

Bull Inn, 43, St. Stephen's street—Matthew Rackham

Crown Inn, 32, Upper Westwick-street—George Rampley

King's Head Inn, 38, St. Giles'—Isaac Seggins

Currier's Arms, 79, St. Giles'—Simpson Robert

Angel Inn, 16, Market-place—John Balls

Elephant Inn, 108, Magdalen-street—Charles Brown

Maid's Head Inn, 1, Fyebridge-street—William Webster

Black Horse Inn, 10, St. Giles' Broad street—J. M. Murry

Black Bull Inn, 11, Magdalen-street—John Clarke

Cock, Rampant Horse-street

George, 15, Hay-market—William Chapman, jun.

Greyhound, Surry-street

Jolly Farmers, Castle-Ditches

Pope's Head, Upper Market street—Thomas Gooch

Rampant Horse, Rampant Horse street

Wheat Sheaf, Bethel-street

Woolpack, St. Giles' Broad-street—Bolton

White Horse, Magdalen-street

Wounded Heart, Upper Market

Names and Residence of Persons having Coaches, Post-Chaises, and Single-Horse Chaises to Let.

Culyer William, Woolpack-yard, St. Giles'—Post Horses

Gowen Thomas, 23, Bethel-street

Richards Edward, 32, Botolph-street—Post Horses

Sparks Britton, 23, Elm-hill—Post Horses, &c.

Sword Benjamin, 6, King-street—Post Horses, Chaises, &c.

Town Daniel, 11, Upper Goat-lane—Post Horses

Woods Wm. 8, Wilkes's lane, near Bank place—Post Horses, &c.

List of Fairs in Norfolk.

ACLE, Midsummer-day	Horning, Monday after August 2
Alburgh, June 21	Ingham, Monday after Whit-Monday
Attleburgh, Th. bef. East. Th. bef. Whit Sun. and Aug. 15	Kenninghall, July 18, Sept. 30 (Sheep Show)
Aylsham, March 23, last Tuesday in Sept. and Oct. 6	Kiptonash (Sheep Show), Sept. 4

Bacton, first Monday in August, November 30	Litcham, Nov. 1
Banham, Jan. 22	Loddon, Easter Monday and Monday after Nov. 22
Binham, July 25	Ludham, Thurs. after Whitsun-week
Briston, May 26	Lynn (Mart), Feb. 14, lasts 8 days—Oct. 16
Broomhill, July 7	Lyng, November 21
Burnham, East. Mon. and Aug. 1	Massingham, Tuesday before Easter, November 8
Castleacre, April 18, July 25	Mattishall, Tuesday before Holy Thursday
Cawston, Feb. 1, and last Wednesday in April and Aug.—Sheep Show	Methwold, April 25
Cley, last Friday in July	New Buckenham, last Saturday in May, and November 22
Coltishall, Whit-Monday	Northwalsham, Holy Thursday
Cressingham Magna, Aug. 12	Northwold, Nov. 30
Cromer, Whit-Monday	Norwich, Day before Good Friday
Dereham, Th. and Fr. before Old Midsummer, and Th. and Fr. before New Michaelmas	Do. (Bishop-Bridge) Easter Monday and Tuesday
Diss, November 8	Do. (do.) Whit Monday and Tuesday
Downham, May 8, Nov. 13	Oxburgh, March 25
Elmham, April 5	Pulham St. Mary, Third Thursday in May
St. Faith's, October 17	Reepham, June 29
Feltwell, November 20	Rudham, May 17, October 14

Fincham, March 3	Scole, Easter Tuesday
Forncett, Sept. 11	Scottow, do.
Foulsham, first, Tuesday in May	Shouldham, Sept. 19, Oct. 10
Frettenham, first Monday in April	Southrepps, July 25
Fring, May 10, December 11	Sprowston (Magdalen), Aug. 2
Gaywood, June 11, at Gaywood, and Oct. 17, kept at Lynn Custom-house Quay	Stoke, December 6
Gissing, July 25	Stowbridge, Saturday after Whitsunday
Gressinghall, December 6	Stratton, Oct. 12
Harleston, July 5, Sept. 9, and Nov. 28, 1 month, for Scotch cattle	Swaffham, May 12, July 21, Nov. 3, (Sheep Shows)
Harling East, May 4, Sept. 16 (Sheep Show), Oct. 24	Thetford, May 14, August 2, September 25
Harpley, July 24	Walsingham, Whit-Monday
Hempnall, Whit Monday, Dec. 11	Watton, July 10, October 10, November 8
Hempton, Whit-Tuesday, Nov. 22	Weasenham, Jan. 25
Heacham, August 3	Worsted, May 12
Hingham, March 7, Whit-Tuesday, October 2	Wymondham, Feb. 2 and May 6, O. S.
Hockham, Easter Monday	Yarmouth, March 28 and 29.
Hockwold, July 25	
Holt, April 25, November 25	

CONCISE HISTORY OF NORWICH. [49]

Its latitude, according to Sir Henry Spelman, is 52 degrees, 45 minutes, North: longitude, 1 degree, 19 minutes, East of the Royal Observatory at Greenwich:—It is 108 miles from London by Newmarket, 114 by Bury St. Edmund's, and 110 by Ipswich and Colchester.

It is rather more than a mile and a half in length, from King-street-gate to Magdalen-gate; and a mile and a quarter in breadth, from Bishop's gate to St. Benedict's gate.

It has thirty-four churches, besides the cathedral, chapels, and dissenting meeting-houses; and is encompassed by a ditch, and the remains of a flint-stone wall, begun in 1294 and finished in 1310, which was flanked with forty towers, in the ancient method of fortification, and had twelve gates for entrances on all sides.

THE CASTLE

Is supposed to have been built by King Canute, the Dane, in 1018; and as far the greater number of his subjects were Saxons, who, at this period, were the first architects, and most probably employed, it is considered as one of the most complete Saxon remains in England.

In confirmation of this opinion, all its ornaments are in the true Saxon style; and the bridge leading to it is unquestionably one of the noblest and most perfect Saxon arches now extant.

The inside, instead of an open yard, was filled up with floors of most magnificent and spacious apartments; traces of which may yet be seen by persons accustomed to examine buildings of this sort. On the ground floor they were vaulted over with stone, for a great part of the old vault still remains; also the great stone arches of the buttresses, and a stone vaulting where the present chapel is. It was used as a prison so early as the reign of Henry I. but not for that purpose solely:—the upper apartments of these towers, were state apartments, for the residence of great officers and their attendants.

Its length is 92 feet, 10 inches; the length of the North and South fronts, 98 feet each: the walls are 50 feet in heighth.

Somewhat resembling the architecture of the Old, is the New Castle, adjoining to it on the East side, built with Scotch granite in the year 1793; apparently of great strength and durability.

The Castle-Hill appears to have been raised by art, with incredible labour: it stands nearly in the center of the city, and commands an agreeable prospect of the surrounding buildings, interspersed with gardens, which, with the adjacent country and river, form a most delightful landscape.

Since the addition of the Gardens round the bottom of the Hill, strangers have acknowledged the view from the summit to be superior to any thing of the kind in Europe, and have justly styled Norwich 'The City in an Orchard.'

In the Shire-House, which adjoins the Castle on the North side, the Summer Assizes and Quarter-Sessions are held, and other county business transacted.

THE CATHEDRAL

Was founded by Bishop Herbert in 1096, and was chiefly composed of wood, which, by various accidents, and the turbulence of the times, was often greatly damaged.

The present Cathedral is a fine Gothic free-stone building, brought to the magnificent state in which it now appears by the bounty of numerous benefactors, at various times, and completed by William Middleton, the thirty-sixth Bishop, in the year 1284. The roof is adorned with various well-carved images, from the historical passages of scripture. On the windows at the East end of the church is most curiously painted the transfiguration, and the twelve apostles, by Dean Lloyd's lady.

The shaft, or spire, is handsome and well proportioned. Except Salisbury, it is the highest in the kingdom, being 105 yards, 2 feet, from the pavement to the top of the pinnacle, strongly built with free-stone on the outside and brick within. The top stone of the spire consists of half a globe, 1 yard, 2 inches broad, with a channel round it; whence extend eight leaves of stone, spreading outward, under which commence the eight rows of crockets, continued down the spire, at 5 feet distance from each other. The weather-cock placed here at the restoration, is three quarters of a yard high, and one yard, two inches broad, as is also the crossbar.

The Cloister on the South side of the church is the largest quadrangle of the kind in England, each side measuring 58 yards in length, near 14 feet in breadth, and 16 feet, 6 inches in heighth;—the stone roof is ornamented with elegant carvings, representing the visions of the Revelations, the Crucifixion and Resurrection, the Legends of St. Christopher, St. Lawrence, &c.

At the South-West corner, the Espousals, or Sacrament of Marriage, are carved in stone, and at the entrance of the Cloister from hence, on the left hand, are the two lavatories, where the monks used to wash their hands. Over one of them is carved a fox in a pulpit, in the habit of a secular priest, holding up a goose to has auditory, intended as a reflection on the secular clergy, or parish priests, to whom the monks bore an inveterate hatred.

On the North side of the Cathedral stands the Bishop's Palace, to which are most elegant gardens.

The Free Grammar school, near this, is a neat, spacious, gothic building, formerly used as a charnel-house.

ST. ANDREW'S HALL,

Formerly the monastery church of the Black Friars, or Benedictine Monks, is a beautiful structure, about 50 yards in length, and 30 in width: the roof is supported by twelve neat and very slender pillars. It was built by Sir Thomas Erpingham, Knt. in 1428; and was the place where the company of St. George used to hold their meetings of business and pleasure.

The Mayor's guild-feast is always held here.

Over a clock, in the center of the East end, is carved the effigies of Justice, and underneath, the royal arms of England. On each side, the pictures of Queen Anne, George Prince of Denmark, Robert Earl of Orford, John Lord Hobart, afterwards Earl of Buckenhamshire, Horatio Walpole, Esq. Lord Suffield, and two Historical Paintings of Edward and Eleonora, and the Death of Lady Jane Grey, by Mr. W. Martin, between which is placed, in a splendid and emblematical frame, a highly-finished portrait of the brave Lord Nelson, painted by Sir William Beachey, with several Aldermen and Benefactors to the city. The figure of St. George killing the dragon, neatly carved, was placed here in 1686, by order of the St. George's Company. On the walls of the North and South ailes are placed elegant paintings at full length, superbly framed, of those Gentlemen who have gone through the public offices of the Corporation with dignity and honour.

Against the further pillar on the North side, is an Ensign, 60 feet in length, supported by a flag-staff, near the top of which is an ornamented Shield, with the following Inscription:

> "The Ensign of the French Ship,
> GENEREUX,
> Taken in the Mediterranean, Feb. 18th, 1800,
> By His Majesty's Ship, Foudroyant, and Squadron,
> Commanded by
> LORD NELSON:
> The Genereux, with the Guillaume Tell, since taken by the
> Foudroyant, Lion, and Penelope, were the only Ships

which escaped the memorable Victory obtained by Lord Nelson over the French, at the Nile, Aug. 1st, 1798.

In testimony of his Gratitude for the Honours conferred on him by the City of Norwich, this Trophy is presented, in the second Mayoralty of Robert Harvey, Esq. by

SIR EDWARD BERRY, KNT.
Captain of his Majesty's Ship, Foudroyant,
1800."

Herein is a handsome room for the city Library, re-built in the Gothic taste, under the direction of the late Mr. Rawlins.

THE GUILD-HALL.

In this Hall, the assizes and quarter sessions for the city are held. Also the Mayor's office, for the daily administration of justice; the town-clerk's and chamberlain's offices: and all elections for Mayor, Aldermen, Sheriffs and Common-councilmen are here determined.

The windows contained many stories on painted or stained glass, relating to the administration of justice;—there now remain perfect only one large and two small windows, to perpetuate the remembrance of this beautiful art.

The room is adorned with the pictures of King William and Queen Mary, many eminent men of the county, mayors of the city, and other benefactors.

Herein is the following inscription, suspended from a Golden Anchor, at the bottom of which are Lord Nelson's arms, neatly executed—in the center *Tria junca in uno*, on one side a Lion, on the other a Sailor, at foot *Faith and Works*.

"The Sword of the Spanish Admiral Don Xavier Winthuysen, who died of the wounds he received in an engagement with the British Fleet under the command of Admiral Earl St. Vincent, 14th Feb. 1797, which ended in the most brilliant victory ever obtained by this Country over the Enemy at Sea: wherein the heroic Valour and cool determined Courage of Rear Admiral Sir Horatio Nelson, K. B. had ample scope for their display. He being a Native of Norfolk, honoured the City by presenting this Sword, surrendered to him in that Action."

The City Prison is directly opposite.

ST. PETER OF MANCROFT CHURCH

Was begun in 1430, and finished in 1455. It is esteemed a very handsome parish church: has a fine square tower steeple, 98 feet high, though designed at first to have been much higher, as appears from the double buttresses reaching to the top, and the thickness of the walls: this tower contains an excellent peal of twelve bells, cast by Messrs. Pack and Chapman, of London, in 1775; the Tenor weighing 41 cwt. The whole is covered with lead, and supported by two rows of pillars, remarkably neat and slender, forming eliptic arches at their top.

The altar-piece, representing the story of St. Peter being delivered out of prison, was painted by that ingenious artist Mr. Catton, and presented to the parish by Alderman Starling, in 1768. The furniture of the altar is crimson velvet, and the plate exceedingly grand, all but one cup being double gilt: one piece of it is remarkably curious, being an elegant standing cup and cover of silver, double gilt, weighing 46 oz. 1 gr. 1 pt. given by Sir Peter Gleane, Knight, whereon is beautifully chased the story of Abigail bringing presents to David.

In the vestry hangs a neat old painted carving in alabaster, of nine female saints, probably designed for some altar of St. Margaret, who is the principal figure, and here represented as holding down a dragon; among others, St. Hilda, holding a book and pastoral staff; St. Barbara, a tower and palm-branch. There is also an octavo manuscript bible upon vellum, written in 1340, and a folio manuscript much more ancient, containing all St. Paul's epistles, with a comment.

THE NORFOLK AND NORWICH HOSPITAL,

St. Stephen's road, is a very neat edifice: was erected in 1772, and is still supported by voluntary contributions.

The Public Library is now kept at the building formerly the Roman Catholic chapel, in Wymer-street, and contains 5000 volumes, where books are delivered by the Librarian to the subscribers every day between the hours of eleven and two, Sundays and the following days excepted, 29th of May, 4th of June, the Guild-day, and the day preceding; 25th of October and 5th of November.

BRIDEWELL,

Was built by Bartholomew Appleyard, about the year 1370. William Appleyard, his son, the first Mayor of Norwich, served his Mayoralty here in 1403. The North wall of this Bridewell is encrusted with cut flints, and is seventy-six feet in length, by about twenty-five high: it is considered one of the greatest curiosities of the kind in England. The flints are squared to such a nicety, that the edge of a knife can scarcely be insinuated between the joints: most of them are about three inches square, the surface is very smooth, and no brick-work can appear more regular.

Several churches and other buildings in the city are thus built.

Mr. Talman says, that the Jews introduced the art of squaring flints: and Dr. Cromwell Mortimer, Secretary to the Royal Society, in a note on a paper of Mr. Arderon's on this very wall, observes, that the gate of the Austin Friars, at Canterbury, that of St. John's Abbey, at Colchester, and the gate near Whitehall, Westminster, are in the same taste. But the platform on the top of the Royal Observatory at Paris, which, in instead of being covered with lead, is paved with flint after this manner, is an instance that the French have in some measure recovered this art. Phil. Trans. Abr. vol. 10. p. 1304.

THE THEATRE

Was built by the late Mr. Thomas Ivory, after the model of old Drury-lane house; and in 1800 underwent an entire, elegant, and spirited alteration, under the direction, and highly to the credit of, the present Patentee, Mr. Wilkins.

The house now contains two circles of Boxes, with side ones on the same tier as the Gallery. There are Stage Boxes the same as those of Drury-lane. The Stage doors are semi-circular, and a Box over them, both of these are filled with a triliage of gold and a small pilaster. The Boxes are supported by small reeded columns of gold, and the front of every Box decorated with coloured Raphael ornaments, on a ground of French grey. At each column are lamps (patent), in the Grecian style, suspended from an antique branch of gold, which gives a brilliancy to the whole. The general tone of colour is a quiet fawn, which is pleasing to the eye, and relieves the pannels of coloured ornaments. The mouldings are gold and white, which give a lightness to the whole. From the entablature or cornice in front, descends a cove, with the Imperial Arms in the centre, admirably executed, painted yellow, and heightened in gold, with this motto, *Conabimur* (we will endeavour); below this is a rich crimson curtain, with gold fringe, supported by two statues, and on each side of the stage doors are pilasters of gold, reeded, in which every reed plays in the light, and produces the most pleasing effect. There are distinct entrances to each part of the house, Boxes, Pit, and Gallery, and the Box Lobbies are roomy and commodious. At the back of the upper circle is a bar-room, where coffee, tea, sweets, &c. may be procured.

The Assembly-Rooms next it are spacious and brilliant.

There are five Hospitals: one of them, St Giles', founded originally for the entertainment of strangers, was, by Henry VIII. appropriated to the poor of the city; which maintains 104 poor men and women, who are all cloathed in grey, and must be sixty years of age. Another for 16 poor men and 8 women, whose livery is purple. Cooke's Hospital, in the Rose-lane, maintains 10 poor women; and Doughty's, which was founded in 1687, supports 24 poor men and 8 women. The Boys and Girls' Hospital contain 30 of each, and the boys are from thence put out apprentices. Besides 5 Charity Schools, where 111 boys and 22 girls are taught, clothed, and supplied with books. A number of Sunday Schools under the care of the Rev. Lancaster Adkin, where 133 boys and girls receive every attention, with many advantages—and several other Charity and Sunday Schools, on foundations, or supported by voluntary contributions from dissenting meetings, &c. taking the whole together, educating, clothing, &c. 300 boys and 150 girls.

The City of Norwich has local advantages superior to most cities in the kingdom: a navigable stream to the port of Yarmouth passes through the middle of it, with great convenience for the Wharfage and Delivery of goods of all kinds to and from London.

It is situated on a mixed soil of ground, in a salubrious air, neither subject to violent or scorching heat, nor to moist or watery vapours. The upper stratum of earth is light soil, of sufficient depth for the plough; the under stratum is chalk, gravel, and sand.

It is happily screened and defended from the Easterly winds by a considerable rising ground, called Moushold Heath, which is higher than the tops of the churches in the lower parts of the city.

If abounds in springs of water of the purest kind, nearly equal to the celebrated Bristol water, supplied to the inhabitants by a variety of public pumps.

The City is governed by a mayor, recorder, steward, 2 sheriffs, 24 aldermen, and 60 common council-men; a town-clerk, sword-bearer, &c. The mayor is elected by the freemen on the first day of May, and sworn into office on the Guild-day, the Tuesday before Midsummer-day; except when Midsummer-day falls on a Wednesday, and then the Guild is kept on the Tuesday se'nnight before Midsummer-day. He is chosen from among the Aldermen, is justice of the quorum during his mayoralty, and afterwards justice of the peace for life.

The sheriffs are also annually elected, one by the Aldermen, the other by the freemen, on the last Tuesday in August, and sworn Sept. 29.

The city is divided into twelve wards, viz. Ber-street, Colegate, North Conisford, South Conisford, Coslany, Fyebridge, Mancroft, St. Giles, St. Stephen, East Wymer, Middle Wymer, Weft Wymer; each of which elects two Aldermen.

These twelve wards are again divided into four great wards;

I. Conisford ward contains South Conisford, North Conisford, Ber-street, with the hamlets of Lakenham, Trowse, Milgate, Bracondale, and Carrowe; which is represented by 12 common council-men.

II. Mancroft ward contains St. Stephen's, St. Peter's of Mancroft, St. Giles', with the hamlet of Eaton; and is represented by 16 common council-men.

III. Wymer ward contains East Wymer, Middle Wymer, West Wymer, with the hamlets of Heigham and Earlham; and is represented by 20 common council-men.

IV. The Northern Ward Coslany, Colgate, Fye-bridge, with the hamlet of Pockthorpe; and is represented by 12 common council-men.

The freemen for each ward elect Three Nominees, and the Nominees appoint the other common council-men.

The city sends two members to parliament, elected by the freeholders and freemen; the latter are free by inheritance, purchase, or servitude, in number about 3000. The freemen must have been admitted to their freedom twelve months before they are entitled to a vote.

The Markets are on Wednesdays and Saturdays.

LIST OF THE COURT OF ALDERMEN OF NORWICH, 1801–1802.

Aldermen's Names.	Time when elected.			In the Room of	Wards.	Sheriff.	Mayor
JEREMIAH IVES, jun. Esq. MAYOR.	September	25,	1779	Sir H. Harbord, Bart.	East Wymer	1782	1786 1801
PAST THE CHAIR.							
R. Harvey, Esq. D. M.	January	5,	1768	Wm. Wigget, Esq.	Coslany	1766	1770 1800
Jeremiah Ives, Esq.	July	1,	1766	Thomas Vere, Esq.	S. Conisford	1763	1769 1795
James Crowe, Esq.	July	18,	1772	Thomas Harvey, Esq.	N. Conisford	1771	1774 1797
Richard Peete, Esq.	January	25,	1773	Robert Harvey, Esq.	W. Wymer	1772	1775
Francis Colombine, Esq.	April	26,	1774	John Wood, Esq.	Colegate	1769	1776
Sir Roger Kerrison, Knt.	October	4,	1774	Richard Matthews, Esq.	Mancroft	1774	1778
John Morse, Esq.	July	1,	1777	Nockold Thompson, Esq.	N. Conisford	1779	1781
Starling Day, Esq.	September	23,	1777	John Nuthall, Esq.	W. Wymer	1775	1782
Jer. I.	January	6,	1779	William	Ber-street	1779	1783

Harvey, Esq.				Crowe, Esq.			
R. Partridge, Esq.	October	6,	1778	Andrew Chamber, Esq.	Ber-street	1780	1784
Elias Norgate, Esq.	January	22,	1779	John Goodman, Esq.	Mancroft	1781	1785
R. Harvey, jun. Esq.	January	21,	1780	James Poole, Esq.	East Wymer	1784	1787
John Patteson, Esq.	December	10,	1781	Sir T. Churchman, Knt.	St. Stephen's	1785	1788
Charles Weston, Esq.	March	15,	1782	John Thurlow, Esq.	Colegate	1785	1789
Thomas Watson, Esq.	June	19,	1783	Thomas Rogers, Esq.	Fyebridge	1787	1790
J. G. Baseley, Esq.	February	20,	1787	Jer. Ives, Esq.	Fyebridge	1789	1791
John Harvey, Esq.	July	24,	1787	John Gay, Esq.	M. Wymer	1784	1792
John Buckle, Esq.	January	15,	1788	Thomas Starling, Esq.	St. Giles'	1787	1793
James Hudson, Esq.	October	18,	1791	Knipe Gobbet, Esq.	St. Giles'	1788	1794
Wm. Herring, Esq.	May	22,	1795	Nathaniel Roe, Esq.	S. Conisford	1786	1796

John Browne, Esq.	March	13,	1798	Charles Weston, Esq.	St. Stephen's	1794	1798
John Herring, Esq.	March	20,	1798	Benj. Day, Esq.	Coslany	1786	1799
BELOW THE CHAIR.							
Mr. Alderman Leman	August	24,	1797	John Addey, Esq.	M. Wymer		

Sheriffs,

THOMAS BACK, Jun. and ROBERT WARD, Esqrs.

CHARLES HARVEY, Esq.—RECORDER.

STEWARD—(*Not yet appointed*).

Common Council

MR. HENRY HARMER, Speaker.

Conisford Ward.—12.			
When first elected.		**When first elected.**	
1772	Mr. James Chase—*Nominee*	1787	Mr. Edward Browne
75	Thos. Dove—*Nominee*	90	Charles Foster
1800	T. Tompson—*Nominee*	96	Henry Gridley
1781	Daniel Bloom	99	Jas. Page Cocksedge
82	Mark Osborn	1801	John Angell, jun.
86	Jacob Smith	1801	Thomas Hawkins
Mancroft Ward.—16.			
1778	Mr. R. Beatniffe—*Nominee*	1799	Mr. J. H. Cole
89	P. Chamberlin—*Nominee*	99	George Stacey
94	Chas. Chamberlin	99	John Horth
98	Jonathan Matchett	1800	James Bennett
98	Arthur Browne	1800	Tho. Barber
98	John Clipperton	1800	James Adams
99	John Stoddart	1801	James Keymer
99	S. Day, jun.	1801	Henry Harmer
Great Wymer Ward.—20.			
1788	Mr. W. Foster, jun.—*Nominee*	1796	Mr James Marsh
88	John Staff—*Nominee*	96	Bosom Roe
89	John Proctor—*Nominee*	97	Samuel Stone
82	Wm. Foster	98	Joseph Stannard
85	Wm. Unthank	98	Samuel Blogg
88	Robert Harmer	98	John Ansell

90	John Lovick	98	Benjamin Bates
91	John Fox	99	John Huggins
91	Christopher Berry	1800	Robert Roe
93	Jonathan Davey	1800	Robert Prentice

Ward beyond the Water.—12.

1795	Mr Cha. Tuthill—*Nominee*	1797	Mr. Edmund Reeve
86	Rob. Powell—*Nominee*	98	Wm. Newson
90	John Brittan—*Nominee*	99	Wm. Burrows
70	James Beevor	1800	Thomas Barnard
99	Wm. Barnard	1800	Joseph Scott
90	Wm. Powell	1801	Peter Wilsea

COMMITTEES IN THE CITY OF NORWICH.

Chamberlain's Council.

Sir Roger Kerrison, John Harvey, James Hudson, and John Browne, Esqrs.—Messrs. James Marsh, Wm. Newton, Wm. Barnard, and Joseph Scott.

Hospital Committee.

J. Crowe, J. Harvey, J. Hudson, and W. Herring, Esqrs. Messrs. W. Foster, W. Barnard, J. Marsh, and H. Harmer.

City Committee.

J. Ives, St. Clement's, R. Harvey, R. Partridge, and J. G. Baseley, Esqrs.—Messrs. W. Foster, jun. Robert Powell, John Brittan, and Jos. Stannard.

Market Committee.

J. Buckle, James Hudson, J. Browne, Esqrs. and Mr. Alderman Leman—Messrs. J. Proctor, J. Ansell, J. Lovick, and Mr. Sheriff Ward.

Clavers.

The Mayor, Mr. Alderman Leman—Mr. Charles Chamberlin, and Mr. Robert Roe.

Auditors.

Francis Colombine, Robert Harvey, jun. John Patteson, and Wm. Herring, Esqrs.—Messrs. Wm. Unthank, James Chase, Wm. Foster, jun. and Charles Tuthill.

Tonnage Committee.

R. Harvey, R. Peete, Esqrs. Sir Roger Kerrison, and Starling Day, Esq.—Messrs. T. Dove, T. Barnard, T. Tompson, and Samuel Stone.

River and Street Committee.

Robert Harvey, John Morse, J. G. Baseley, and Wm. Herring, Esqrs.—Messrs. Edward Browne, John Staff, Charles Foster, and John Fox.

Committee for inspecting the Assembly Bonds.

J. I. Harvey, C. Weston, T. Watson, and J. Browne, Esqrs.—Messrs. S. Stone, H. Gridley, S. Blogg, and Wm. Burrows.

Coal Committee.

Jer. Ives, St. Clement's, John Morse, J. I. Harvey, and John Greene Baseley, Esqrs.—Messrs. W. Powell, Christopher Berry, Jonathan Matchett, and Benjamin Bates.

Committee of Appeals to the River Water Assessments.

(BY THE ASSEMBLY.)	(BY THE LESSEES.)
R. Partridge, Esq.	Mr. Daniel Ganning
John Herring, Esq.	John Webb
Mr. John Procter	John Cozens
Arthur Browne	Thomas Hawkins

TREASURERS of the several HOSPITALS, &c.

Great Hospital	Sir Roger Kerrison.
Doughty's Hospital	Robert Harvey, Esq.
Boy's Hospital	Charles Weston, Esq.
Girl's Hospital	R. Harvey, jun. Esq.
Court Bonds	Sir Roger Kerrison.
Assembly Bonds	Charles Weston, Esq.
Tonnage	Sir Roger Kerrison.
City Lamps	Robert Harvey, jun. Esq.

Mr. Stephen Aldhouse, Surgeon to the Four Hospitals.

Mr. B. Bird, Steward to the Estates of the same.

OFFICERS of the CORPORATION.

E. De Hague, Gent. Town Cl.	Messrs. A. Taylor, jun. and J. Marsh—Under Sheriffs
W. Simpson, Gent. Chamberl	Mr. W. Mack, Ch. Constable
T. Marks, Esq. Coroner	Mr. Rich. Harman, Clerk of the Market
Jas. Marsh, Gent. Coroner	Mr. J. Dunham, Water Bailiff
Mr. Thos. Lubbock, Sword-bearer	Mr. Samuel Cole, jun. Inspector of Corn Returns

Mr. Joshua Lawter, Under-Chamberlain	

CITY SURGEONS.

Mr. Robert Scott

Mr. James Keymer

Mr. James Robinson

The City Surgeons are also Men-Midwives in their respective Districts.

The CORPORATION of GUARDIANS of the POOR in NORWICH.

CHARLES HARVEY, Esq. Governor.

ROBERT PARTRIDGE, Esq. Deputy Governor.

ROBERT HARVEY, Esq. Treasurer.

The MAYOR, RECORDER, STEWARD, SHERIFFS, and ALDERMEN for the time being.

For the Great Ward of Conisford, Ber-street, and Trowse.	
Elected in 1800.	Elected in 1801.
Edward Squire, corn-merch.	Edw. Browne, carpenter
James Chase, liquor-merch.	Francis Sillis, farmer
Thomas Dove, carpenter	John Angell, jun. currier
Thos. Tompson, merchant	Mark Osborn, grocer
For the Great Ward of Mancroft.	
Rich. Beatniffe, bookseller	John C. Hampp, merchant
Thomas Back, backer	Peter Chamberlin, grocer
Wm. Burt, upholder	Samuel Harmer, Gent.
John Athow, stone-mason	Mr. Sheriff Ward
For the Great Ward of Wymer.	
Jas. Buttivant, manufacturer	John Rodwell, dyer
Richard Bacon, printer	Samuel Blogg, mason

William Unthank, Gent.	Wm. Foster, jun. Gent.
Jonathan Davey, merchant	James Marsh, Gent.
For the Ward beyond the Water.	
William Cutting, merchant	John Brittan, woolcomber
James Angier, merchant	John Webb, woolcomber
Robert Powell, woolcomber	Wm. Barnard, merchant
Edward Reeve, grocer	Joseph Scott, merchant

Mr. WILLIAM SIMPSON, Clerk of the Court.

Mr. J. SWIFT, Beadle.

Mr. Thomas Nichols, Assistant Beadle.

C. Church, Removal Officer.

C. Church, Mayor's Constable.

T. Warren and J. Simonds, Visitors.

N.B. General Courts of the Guardians are held on the first Tuesday in every Month, at Three o'clock in the afternoon, at the Hall in St. Andrew's; and weekly Committees at St. Andrew's Workhouse, every Friday in the Afternoon, and at St. John's Workhouse, every Monday in the Afternoon.

COURT of REQUEST or CONSCIENCE.

The Commissioners are such of the Court of Aldermen and Common Council as qualify themselves according to the Act.

Mr. SAMUEL KING, Register and Clerk.

OFFICE in St. Clement's Church-yard.

The Court is held every Monday before one Alderman and two of the Common Council, in St. Andrew's Hall, at Three o'clock in the afternoon.

EXCISE-OFFICE, ST. GEORGE'S TOMBLAND.

Wm. Carter, Esq. Collector.—Mr. Wm. Flint, Supervisor.

Mr. J. King, Office-keeper.—Mr. T. Sowter, First Clerk.

FIRE INSURANCE OFFICES.

Norwich Insurance-Office, Mr. Adam Taylor, jun. Hog-hill, Secretary.

Union Office, Mr. Thomas Bignold, Gentleman's Walk, Market-place, Secretary.

Agent to the Sun Fire-Office. Mr. John Taylor, at the Glass-warehouse of the late Mr. Cook, St. Andrew's.

Royal-Exchange Office, Mr. John Woodrow, St. George's Colegate.

Phœnix Office, Mr. John Steward, Surry-street.

GOVERNORS of BETHEL.

JEREMIAH IVES, Esq. St. Clement's, PRESIDENT

Jere. Ives, Esq. Catton	Mr. John Gurney
William Herring, Esq.	Sigismund Trafford, Esq.
William Foster, Gent.	Rev. Robert Parr

Treasurer, Mr. John Gurney.

Physicians, Dr. Beevor and Dr. Manning.

Surgeon and Apothecary, Mr. James Keymer.

Clerk and Steward, Mr. Charles Nelson, Land-Surveyor, Red

Lion lane.—Mr. James Bullard, Master.

N.B. The Committee Day is the first Monday in every Month.

Names of the Bishop, Dean, and Prebendaries.

BISHOP.
Right Reverend CHARLES MANNERS SUTTON, D.D.
Palace.

DEAN.
JOSEPH TURNER, D.D. Deanry.

CHANCELLOR.
The Rev. G. Sandby, D.D. at Denton, Norfolk.

PREBENDARIES.

Philip Wodehouse, M.A. Hingham.

John Pretyman, D.D. Norwich.

Robert Potter, A.M. Lowestoft.

Edward South Thurlow, A.M. Norwich.

George Anguish, A.M. Gisleham, Suffolk.

Jos. Procter, D.D. Vice Chancellor of Cambridge.

BISHOP'S OFFICE in the Upper Close.

Deputy Register, C. Kitson, Gent. Notary Public and Proctor, Norwich.

Proctors. William Utten, John Morphew, Charles Kitson, John Steward.

Principal Apparitor, Robert Starkey, Gent.

DEAN and CHAPTER'S OFFICE, in the Cloister.

Clerk and Register, Mr. Wm. Utten.

ARCHDEACON of NORWICH, his OFFICE,

At Mr. Morphew's, King-street.

MEMBERS of PARLIAMENT for NORWICH,

Right Hon. William Windham, Vauxhall.

John Frere, Esq. Spring-Gardens.

Receiver of the land Tax, Sir Roger Kerrison.

Receiver of the Stamp Duty, J. H. Cole, Esq.—His Deputy, Mr. Samuel Cole. The Stamp-office, in St. Giles' Broad-street.

T. Moore, Gent. Bethel-street, Licencer of Hawkers and Pedlars.

Commissions of Appeal under the Income Act.

Robert Fellowes, Esq. Sir Thomas Beevor, Bart. and James Mingay, Esq.— Mr. Adam Taylor, jun. Secretary.

POST OFFICE.

GEORGE LITCHFIELD, GENT.—POST-MASTER.
His Clerk Mr. G. CHAPMAN.

The Mails from London arrive every forenoon about eleven o'clock, except Mondays, and are dispatched every afternoon at half past four, except Saturdays.

The Mails from Huntingdon, Cambridge, Newmarket, Bury, Thetford, &c. arrive, and are dispatched every day at the above time.

The Mails from all the intermediate places betwixt London and Ipswich, betwixt Ipswich and this city and their branches, arrive every day at twelve at noon, and are dispatched to those parts every day at four in the afternoon.

The Mails arrive from Yarmouth every afternoon at four, and are dispatched every day at twelve.

The Mails from Cromer, Aylsham and North Walsham, arrive *every day* at ten in the morning, and are dispatched to those places at one in the afternoon.

N.B. The Office is opened for the delivery of letters about an hour after the arrival of the different Mails, and is shut *at half-past three precisely.*

NORFOLK and NORWICH HOSPITAL.

OFFICERS of the CHARITY.

ROBERT FELLOWES, Esq. Treasurer.

Physicians and Surgeons who attend gratis.

Physicians.	Surgeons.	Assistant Surgeons.
Dr. Manning	Mr. Donne	Mr. Colman
Dr. Hooke	Mr. Rigby	Mr. Aldhouse
Dr. Lubbock	Mr. Martineau	Mr. Bond
Dr. Alderson		

Mr. Thomas Barber, Secretary.—Mr. George Hardy, Apothecary.—Mrs. Isabella Grant, Matron.

The Physicians and Surgeons attend in turn to take in patients, every Saturday at eleven o'clock in the forenoon; and every Tuesday at the same hour, to prescribe to the out-patients.

REGULAR LODGES OF FREE MASONS.

PROVINCIAL   GRAND   MASTER,
WM. EARLE BULWER, ESQ.

R. Partridge, Esq. P.D.G.M. Tho. Marks, Gent. P.S.G.W.

J. Harvey, Esq. P.J.G.W. Jas. Boyce, P.G.S.

No.	
16	White Swan, St. Peter's, Norwich, the first Wednesday in the Month, constituted May 11, 1724.
48	King's Head, Market-place, Norwich, 2d Frid. 1736.
76	King's Head, Yarmouth, Monday nearest the full moon.
78	Angel, Norwich, second Friday, January 5, 1748
80	Horse and Groom, Norwich, first Tuesday, 1749
86	Greenland Fishery, St. Mary's, Norwich, 2d Tues. 1750
88	Three Tuns, Yarmouth, last Wednesday, June 6, 1751
99	Jolly Farmers, Castle Meadow, Norwich, third Tuesday, Nov. 20, 1753.—*Faithful Lodge.*
105	Castle, Norwich, second Thursday, March 13, 1757
120	The Wounded Heart, St. Peter's, Norwich, the fourth Tuesday, Sept. 16, 1766.
133	Norwich Volunteer, All Saints, Norwich, 2d Wednesday.—*Lodge of Friendship.*
136	King's Head, Coltishall, Norfolk, the Wednesday on or nearest the full moon, February 18, 1758
158	Lodge of Friendship, Crown, Lynn Regis, Norfolk, second Friday, from Sept. to May, June 9, 1762
192	Gate House, Tombland, Norwich, the last Wednesday, Feb. 11, 1766
531	Half Moon, Market-place, Yarmouth, on the Monday nearest the full moon, Oct. 7, 1793. *Lodge of Unity.*
552	Maid's Head, Lynn, constituted April 25, 1796, the first Thursday.—

	Lodge of Strict Benevolence.
563	Angel Inn, second Friday, June 26, 1797.—*Norwich Theatrical Lodge.*
564	Shakspeare, Yarmouth, second Friday, June 26, 1797.—*United Friends of Great Yarmouth.*
572	Green Dragon, Grass-market, Lynn, the 2d Thursday, Sept. 28, 1798.—*Lodge of Attention.*

THE POPULATION OF NORWICH,

As taken from the Parochial Returns in the years 1801, 1786, 1752, and 1693.

Parishes.	Inhab. Houses.	No. of families	Uninha Houses	Total Souls	Souls in 1786	Souls in 1752	Souls in 1693
St. Peter Southgate	102	132	21	378	507	425	470
St Etheldred	64	66	4	252	254	247	243
St. Julian	191	197	20	662	846	595	593
St Peter Permountergate	298	311	18	1350	1362	1408	1376
St. John Sepulchre	292	303	20	1144	1114	1004	781
St. Michael at Thorn	353	361	49	1198	1442	1127	865
St. John Timberhill	228	237	3	888	975	890	668
All Saints	172	199	4	701	825	578	425
St. Stephen	509	573	32	2211	2360	2314	1769
St. Peter Mancroft	441	493	19	2120	2299	2288	1953
St. Giles	235	270	4	1076	1117	961	910
St. Benedict	198	238	29	830	900	715	652
St. Swithin	113	138	7	503	643	751	496
St. Margaret	151	186	22	662	859	856	664
St. Lawrence	245	248	24	899	1018	952	668
St. Gregory	212	362	9	1057	1113	1202	772
St. John Maddermarket	148	176	12	1698	1571	1107	657

St. Andrew	224	236	11	1858	1773	1334	935
St. Michael at Plea	72	80	5	446	502	482	479
St. Peter Hungate	85	103	3	371	394	341	269
St. George Tombland	127	186	8	750	720	737	722
St. Simon and Jude	77	83	6	333	443	420	362
St. Martin at Palace	226	264	27	936	1109	1083	819
St. Helen	74	74	6	393	446	386	338
St. Michael Coslany	224	261	31	1031	1185	1046	1026
St. Mary	277	303	29	1018	1202	1178	949
St. Martin at Oak	336	413	34	1747	2153	1698	1243
St. Augustine	327	338	75	1232	1899	1226	850
St. George Colegate	246	293	37	1132	1272	1295	1154
St. Clement	135	193	11	853	800	816	593
St. Edmund	90	137	9	446	531	520	370
St. Saviour	203	235	22	984	593	810	701
St. Paul	323	375	55	1395	1681	1461	983
St. James	228	149	23	520	608	696	416
Pockthorpe	214	255	27	979	1272	1116	732
Heigham	213	215	14	854	923	653	544
HAMLETS.							
Lakenham	84	89	5	428	486	165	221

Eaton	36	57	2	278	260	226	153
Earlham	12	12	0	95	66	68	50
Hellesdon	16	16	1	81	108	70	65
Thorpe	17	17	0	74	82	36	69
Trowse, Carrowe, Bracon	83	88	6	353	348	386	258
Precinct of the Close	156	136	3	616		700	650
TOTAL,	8026	9093	747	36832	40051	36196	28881

The decrease in the population of this City, since 1786, is 3219; but it is to be observed that 1786 was a year of peace, and that in the returns of 1801, those serving in the Navy, Army, and Militia, are not included. Norwich, during the present war, has furnished, at least, 4000 recruits.

COACHES, BARGES, and WAGGONS, to and from NORWICH.

THE MAIL CARRIAGES

Set out every day from the King's Head, in the Market-place, Norwich; from the Swan with Two Necks, Lad-lane, and Golden-Cross, Charing-Cross London. Half an hour allowed at Thetford and Ipswich, both in going up and coming down; fourteen pounds luggage to each passenger, and all above, two-pence per pound.

Parcels delivered immediately on their arrival at London and Norwich.

Passengers for these carriages should be at the Golden-Cross at Seven; and at the Swan at half past seven; or at the General Post-Office, Lombard-street, just before eight o'clock in the evening.

The MAIL COACH by Ipswich, arrives at the King's Head Inn, Norwich, at twelve o'clock at noon, and sets out at four in the afternoon; stops for breakfast coming down, and for supper going up, at Bamford's, the Great White Horse, Ipswich.

The MAIL COACH by Newmarket, arrives at the King's Head Inn, Norwich, about eleven o'clock in the morning, and sets out at half past four in the afternoon; stops for breakfast coming down, and for supper going up, at Radcliffe's, the Bell, at Thetford.—Each carriage is well lighted, and guarded through the whole of the journey by persons who are also experienced drivers.

The MAIL COACH to YARMOUTH (in three hours), sets out from the King's Head Inn, Market-place, Norwich, and Star Tavern, on the Quay, Yarmouth, every day at twelve o'clock. By this Coach, passengers and parcels are likewise booked throughout from Yarmouth to London.

From the Golden Cross, Charing Cross, and Swan, Lad-lane, are mail and other carriages to every part of the kingdom.

The EXPEDITION, by NEWMARKET,

A double-bodied coach, sets out from the White Swan, St. Peter's, Harwich, every afternoon at three o'clock, to the White Horse, Fetter-lane, London; returns from the above Inn daily, at half past three o'clock; calls at the Bull, Bishopgate-street, going out and coming in.

The STAGE COACH, by BURY,

Sets out every Monday and Wednesday, at three in the afternoon, and on Saturday at half pair three, from the Angel, in the Market-place, Norwich;

and every Tuesday, Thursday, and Sunday, from the Swan with Two Necks, Lad-lane, London, at four in the afternoon.

LYNN and NORWICH EXPEDITION,
By WAY of SWAFFHAM and DEREHAM,

Sets out from the Crown Inn, Lynn, every Monday, Wednesday, and Friday morning, at seven o'clock, to the White-Swan, in St. Peter's Norwich; returns from the Swan every Tuesday, Thursday, and Saturday morning, at the same hour. In November, December, and January, this coach goes only on Tuesdays and Saturdays.

YARMOUTH MACHINE,

From the Black Horse, on Tombland, to the Wrestlers in Yarmouth, sets out twice every day, Saturday excepted, at eight o'clock in the morning, and three in the afternoon, during the summer, and at nine o'clock each morning in the winter season only.

N.B. For about two months in the worst part of the winter season the coach goes once a day only.

The LONDON and NORWICH STAGE WAGGONS,

By Messrs. William Mack and Co. St. Giles' Broad-street, to the Green Dragon, Bishopsgate-street, set out from Norwich every Monday and Friday evening, and come in every Monday and Thursday morning.

Messrs. Robert and I. L. Marsh and Sons' LONDON, CAMBRIDGE, and NORWICH WAGGONS, set out every Tuesday, Wednesday, and Friday Evening, and arrive every Monday, Tuesday, and Thursday morning. As they constantly pass through Cambridge, there is now a regular Conveyance to York, Manchester, Birmingham, Sheffield, and all the Manufacturing Towns in Yorkshire.

Hadfield's Old York Waggon is now removed to their Warehouse on Tombland.

BURY WAGGON,

From the Star in the Market place, Norwich, comes in on Friday morning, and sets out in the afternoon of the same day.

YORK WAGGONS,

From the Star, in the Market-place, Norwich, in and out every Tuesday and Friday.

LYNN WAGGON,

From the Black Horse, in St. Giles', comes in and goes out every Wednesday and Saturday.

BARGES.

The Old Barge goes from the Wherry Staithe, every Monday and Thursday, for Yarmouth, at ten o'clock, and returns on Tuesday and Friday.

The New Barge goes from the Old Staithe, every Monday and Thursday, for Yarmouth, at ten o'clock, and returns on Tuesday and Friday.

LONDON TRADERS to and from YARMOUTH.

FROM SYMOND'S WHARF.	FROM SMART'S QUAY.
Astley, John Elland	Ceres, Robert Lee
Dove, J. P. Horne	Constant Trader, J. Plowman
New Fair Trader, C. Stewart	Hannah, M. Marshall
Isabella, Charles Taylor	Thomas and Fanny, J. Ferritt
Earl of Leicester, J. Nichols	Yarmouth, James Haill
Providence, R. B. Theobald	Commerce, R. Mansfield
Susanna, Elias Miles	
AGENTS.	AGENTS.
Mr. Cole, Norwich	Mr. Story, Norwich
Mr. J. Dryden, Yarmouth	Mr. James Laws, Yarmouth

HULL TRADERS.

Hope,	John Hepworth
Good Intent,	John Wilkinson
Expedition,	James Metcalf

There are eleven Packets from Yarmouth to Cuxhaven, one of which sails from Yarmouth every Sunday and Thursday morning at nine o'clock.

LIST OF CARRIERS.

Towns.	Miles	Carr. Names.	Where they set up.	Towns they carry parcels for.	Time of comg. in	Time of going out	
ACLE	11	Driver	Golden Lion, St. John's M.	Thorpe, Blofield, Freethorpe, &c.	S	S	1
		Church	Black Horse, Tombland	Thorpe, Blofield, Bullingham, Lingwood,			
Filby, &c.	W S	W S	2				
Aldburgh	15	Grand	Golden Lion, St. John's M.	St. Faith's, Stratton Strawless, Aylsham, &c.	S	S	1
		Fox	Black Horse, Tombland	St. Faith's, Aylsham, Ingworth, Erpingham, &c.	F evg.	S	12
		Randall	Black Horse, St. Giles'	Aylsham, Ingworth, Erpingham, Alby, &c.	S	S	12
Alderford	8		Reepham Carrier				
Ashwelthorpe	9	Brown	Red Lion, Red Lion-lane	Swardeston, Mulbarton, Braconash, Hethel	W S	W S	2
Attlebridge	8		Fakenham Carrier				
Attleburgh	15	Rose	George, Hay-market	Wyndham, Old Buckenham, Beesthorpe, Morley, and Ellingham	W S	W S	1
		Hewitt	Lamb, Hay-market	Wyndham, New Buckenham, Ellingham, and Snetterton	W S	W S	1
Antingham	25		Southrepps Carrier				
Aslacton	12		Long Stratton Carrier				
Aylsham	11	Palmer	Wounded Heart,	St. Faith's, Stratton	W S	W S	12

			Up. mark.	Strawless, Marsham, &c.			
Bacton	18	Watts	Bull, Magdalen-street	Sprowston, Wroxham, Worstead, &c.	F. evg.	S	1
Barningham	16			Gresham Carrier			
Barton Mills	41			London Wagons			
Beccles	18	Woolner	Star, Market-place	Loddon, Lowestoft, Thurlton, Gillingham, &c.	M F	Tu S	12
		Mayhew	White Hart, St. Peter's	Loddon, Lowestoft, &c.	M F	Tu S	2
Blakeney	25			Holt Carrier			
Blickling	13			Aylsham Carrier			
Blofield	6			Acle Carrier			
Booton	11	Allden	Moon & Stars, St. M. Cos.	Felthorpe, Swannington, Reepham, and Sall	W S	W S	1
Botesdale	27	Bidwell, Nunn	Pope's Hd. Mrk. Lamb Mrk.	Long Stratton, Scole, Ixworth, and Bury	Th F e.	F S	10 11
Braconash	6			Ashwellthorpe Carrier			
Bradfield	16			Southrepps Carrier			
Braintree	74			Stowmarket Carrier			
Briston	17	Martin	Moon and Stars, St. Mich.	Heydon, Dawling, Swanton, &c	F	S	10
		Dunn	Recruiting Sergt. St. Mary's	Heydon, Saxthorpe, &c.	Tu evg.	W	11
Brockdish	24	Johnson	Wool-pack, St. Giles'	Pulham, Stradbrook, Wallworth, Brundish, &c.	F evg.	S	11
Brooke	7			Bungay Carrier			
Buckenham	15	Orford	White Hart, St. Peter's	Banham, Wrenningham, Taccolnestone, Forncett,	F	S	11

				Carlton, Old Buckenham, &c.				
Bungay	14	Rayner	Star, Market-place	Brooke, Saxmundham, &c.	M F	Tu S	12	
		Day	Lamb, Market-place	Brooke, Earlham, Woodton, &c.	Tu F	W S	12	
Bunwell	11		Carlton Rode Carrier					
Burlingham	8		Acle Carrier					
Bury St. Ed.	43	Palmer	White Hart, St. Peter's	Wyndham, Attleleburgh, Market Harling, Hapton, Barningham, &c.	Th	F	2	
		Moulton	Wounded Heart, St. Peter's	Long Stratton, Scole, Botesdale, Malborough, Stanton, Ixworth, &c.	F	S	12	
Burnham	38	Holmes	Currier's Arms, St. Giles'	Drayton, Fakenham, Creak, Middleton, &c.	W	W	4	
Cambridge	63		London Waggons					
Carlton Rode	13	Briggs	White Lion, St. Peter's	Mulbarton, Taccolnestone, Buckenham &c.	W S	W S	12	
Castleacre	28		Watton Carrier					
Caston	18		Ellingham Carrier					
Catfield	15	Page	Crown, St. George's	Sprowston, Rackheath, Wroxham, Hoveton, Horning, Hickling &c.	W S	W	4	
Cawston	11	Thurlow	King's Head, St. George's	Felthorpe, Heveringland, Brandestone &c.	W	W S	2	
		Sandall	Ringers, St. Michael's	Horsford, Haveringland, Brandestone &c.	W S	W S	1	
Cley	25		Holt Carrier					

Coltishall	7	Leeds	Pope's Head, Upper-market	Horstead, Scottow, Belaugh, &c.	M W S	M W S	3
		Cooke	Duke's Palace	Crostwick, Horstead, Tunstead, Scottow, Belaugh, &c.	M W S	M W S	3
Colchester	62		London Waggons				
Cromer	21	Adcock	Duke's Palace	Aylsham, Northrepps, &c.	W S	W S	12
		Craske	do.	Aylsham, Gunton, Roughton, Buston, &c.	W S	W	2
Crostwick	5		Coltishall Carrier				
Dereham	16	Fox	Pope's Head, Upper-market	Easton, Honingham, Hockering, Tuddenham, Litcham, Massingham, & Bircham	M F	S	2
		Dunn	Woolpack, St. Giles'	Tuddenham, Hockering, Gressenhall, Yaxham, Swaffham, Castleacre, Lynn	Tu F	W S	12
		Watts	Black Horse, St. Giles'	Do. Wendling, and Fransham	Tu Th S	Tu Th S	12
Dickleburgh	18		Diss Carrier				
Dilham	13	Amis	Elephant, Magdalen-street	East Ruston, Honing, Walcot, Beeston, Smallborough, Dilham, Stowley	S	S	1
Diss	22	Holmes	Star, Market-place	Long Stratton, Dickleburgh, and Ipswich	Tu F	W S	12
		Mason	Rampant Horse, St. Steph.	Long Stratton, Dickleburgh, Scole, Ipswich, and Bury	Tu ev	W	12
Docking	40		Thornham Carrier				

Downham	42	Carter	White Lion, St. Benedict's	Dereham, Swaffham, Wisbech, Spalding, Baston, and Peterburgh	W evg.	Th	6 m.
Earsham	13		Harleslon Carrier				
Easton	5		Mattishall Carrier				
Edgfield	18	Green	White Horse, St. Lawrence	Horsford, Caston Woodrow, &c.	F evg.	S	11
Ellingham	14		Attleburgh Carrier				
Elmham	18	Amis	Wounded Heart, St. Peter's	Litcham, Lexham, Brisley, Stanfield, &c.	F	S	12
		Strutt	Lobster	Drayton, Attlebridge, Morton, Billingford, &c.	W evg.	S	2
Erpingham	16	Dyke	King's Head, Magdalen str.	St. Faith's, Hevingham, Marsham, Aylsham, Ingworth, Calthorpe, Coleby &c.	S	S	2
Eye	18	Rayson	Woolpack, St. Giles'	Hoxne, Stradbrook, Claydon, Thorndon, Stalham, &c.	F evng.	S	11
Fakenham	25	Mitchell	White Hart, St. Peter's	Hellesdon, Drayton, Bawdeswell, Foxley, Stibbard, &c.	Th evg.	F	2
Felbrigg	18		Cromer Carrier				
Felmingham	13		Southrepps Carrier				
Field Dalling	22		Wells Carrier				
Forncett	11	Moore	Two Quarts, St. Stephen's	Taccolnestone, &c.	S	S	2
Foulsham	18	Sewell	Wounded Hart, St. Peter's	Hellesdon, Drayton, Attlebridge,	F	S	12

				Sparham, Bawdeswell, Foxley, &c.			
Foxley	15		Foulsham Carrier		S	S	12
Freethorpe	11	Hubbard	White Lion, St. Mart. Pal.	Brundall, Cantley, &c.	F evng.	S	12
Fressingfield	24	Barrett	Greyhound, St. Stephen's	Trowse, Brooke, Wattle, Lexfield, Hedenham, Harston, Weybread, Stradbrook, Framlingham, &c.			
Garboldisham	20	Smith	Crown, St. Stephen's	Mulbarton, Bracon, Ashwelthorpe, Bunwell, Buckenham, &c.	S	S	3
Grantham	126		York Waggons				
Gresham	22	Burton	Wounded Heart, St. Peter's	Barningham, Baconsthorpe, Alburgh, Aylsham, Itteringham, Plumstead, Matlock, Gresham, Wickmere, &c.	F evng.	S	12
Gunton	17		Southrepps Carrier				
Harleston	20	Palgrave	White Heart, St. Peter's	Brooke, Hedenham, Earsham, Redenhall, Denton, Wattle, Weybread, and Aldborough	F	S	12
		Larter	Pope's Head, Upper-market	Stratton, Pulham, Fersfield, Mendham, &c.	Tu	W	11
Halesworth	23	Garland	White Heart, St. Peter's	Brooke, Bungay, &c.	F	S	11
Halifax	218		York Waggons				
Halstead	61		Stowmarket Carrier				

Hapton	8	Walker	George, Haymarket	Swardeston, Mulbarton, Bracon, Forncett, Tharston, Stratton, and Tasborough	S	S	2
Harling	21		Kenninghall Carrier				
Halvergate	13	Tills	Jolly Farmers, St. Mar. Pa.	Burlingham, Moulton, Freethorpe, Tunstall, and Wickhampton	S	S	3
Hevingham	8	Hill	Shoulder of Mutton, St. Aug.	St. Faith's, &c.	S	S	3
Heveringland	9		Cawston Carrier				
Hardwick	12	Ray	Cock, St. Stephen's	Long Stratton, &c.	W S	W S	1
		Coppin	Nag's Head, St. Stephen's	Newton, Long Stratton, Tasburgh, &c.	W S	W S	1
Hedenham	12		Bungay Carrier				
Hempnall	10	Shreeve	Red-Lion, Red-Lion lane	Lakenham, Stoke, Castor, Shottisham, &c.	S	S	2
Hetherset	5	Bailey	Two Quarts, St. Stephen's	Eaton, &c.	S	S	4
Heydon	14		Cawston Carrier				
Hickling	16	Morter	Cat and Fiddle, Mag. str.	Wroxham, Smallburgh, Stalham, &c.	F evng.	S	1
		Money	Bull, ditto	Stalham, Beeston, Smallburgh, &c.	F evng.	S	12
Hindringham	22	Thompson	Wounded Heart, St. Peter's	St. Faith's, Stratton Strawless, Hevingham, Saxthorpe	Tu	W	12
Hindolveston	18		Foulsham Carrier				
Hingham	14		Watton Carrier				
Hockham	19	Rust	Cock, St. Stephen's	Wyndham, Attleborough, Ellingham,	E evng.	S	12

				Rockland, Stow, Harling, &c.			
Hockering	10		Dereham Carrier				
Holkham	29		Wells Carrier				
Holt	21	Wade		Aylsham, Blakeney, Cley, &c.	Tu evg.	Th	6m
		Spencer	Pope's Head, Upper-market	Aylsham, Edgefield, Saxthorpe, Thornage, Cley, &c.	F	S	10
Honingham	7		Dereham Carrier				
Horning	9		Ludham Carrier				
Houghton	33		Thornham Carrier				
Hoxne	22		Eye Carrier				
Ingham	18	Wagg	King's Head, Magdalen st.	Sprowston, Rackheath, Wroxham, Beeston, Stalham, Ingham, Happisburgh, Smallburgh, &c.	S	S	2
Ingworth	12	Newstead	Bull, Magdalen-street	St. Faith's, Hevingham, Marsham, Aldborough, Calthorpe, &c.	S	S	11
Ipswich	43	Green	Currier's Arms, St. Giles'	Dickleburgh, Brockford, Colchester, Woodbridge, Harwich, Dedenham, &c.	Tu evng.	W	12
Itteringham	15		Holt Carrier				
Ixworth	35		Bury Carriers				
Kenninghall	20	West	Greyhound, St. Stephen's	Swardeston, Bracon, Ashwelthorpe, Buckenham, Market Harling, Garboldisham, Market Weston, North and South Lopham,	F	S	10

				Ixworth, and from thence to Bury			
Knapton	16	Mack	Elephant, Magdalen-street	Coltishall, Scottow, North Walsham, Paston, Trunch, Gillingham	F evg.	S	10
Lammas	9	Kenney	Bull, Magdalen-street	Frettenham, Spixworth, Buxton, &c.	W S	W S	3
Leeds	191		York Waggons				
Lingwood	8		Acle Carrier				
Litcham	24		Lynn Carrier				
Loddon	9	Hardy	Greyhound, St. Stephen's	Framlingham, Yelverton, Thurlton, Langley, &c.	S	S	2
Long Stratton	10	Wright	Cock, St. Stephen's	Newton, Tasburgh, Forncet, &c.	W S	W S	1
Ludham	14	Pert	Cat and Fiddle, Mag. str.	Rackheath, Wroxham, Horning, &c.	S	S	1
Lynn	42	Tuck	Black Horse, St. Giles'	Gressenhall, Elmham, Briston, Litcham, Castleacre, Gayton, Wisbech, Spalding, &c.	W S	W S	5
		Reeder	Wounded Heart, Up. mark.	Easton, Honingham, Hockering, Tuddenham, Attling, Dereham, Scarning, Wendling, Necton, Swaffham, Bilney, and Middleton	W	Th	12

		Coe	Wool-pack, St. Giles'	Shipdham, Swaffham, &c.	M evg.	Tu	11
		Brooke	Wounded Heart, St. Peter's	Gressenhall, Elmham, Litcham, Castleacre, Brisley, Stanfield, Mileham, Wellingham, Guyton, Wisbech, and Peterburgh	F	S	12
Maidenbridge	8			Swanton Carrier			
Marsham	10	Sutton	Crown, St. George's	St. Faith's, Stratton Strawless, Hevingham, &c.	S	S	3
Mattishall	11	Stewart	Prince of Wales, St. Benct.	Easton, East Tuddenham, Honingham, &c.	W S	W S	2
		Howes	Woolpack, St. Giles'	East Tuddenham, &c.	W S	W S	12
		Allen	Sun and Anchor, St. Clem.	East Tuddenham, Honingham, &c.	S	S	3
Mendham	20	Flaxman	Rampant Horse, St. Steph.	Framlingham, Barrow, &c.	S	S	1
Mildenhall	42		London Waggons				
Moulton	13	Randall	Shoulder of Mutton, St. Ste.	Swardeston, Tasburgh, and Long Stratton	S	S	3
Morley	12		Attleborough Carrier				
Mulbarton	5		Ashwelthrope Carrier				
Mundesley	18		Southrepps Carrier				
Necton	24	Drake	Wounded Heart, Upp. mar.	Mattishall, Shipdham,	F	S	12

				Yaxham			
Neatishead	11	Smith	White Horse, Magdalen-str.	Sprowston, Rackheath, and Wroxham	S	S	3
Needham	38		Stowmarket Carrier				
Newmarket	50		London Waggons				
Newton	6		Long Stratton Carrier				
N. Walsham	14	Bentley	Duke's Palace	Catton, Crostwick, Horstead, Coltishall, and Scottow	W S	W S	2
Oulton	14	Kidd	Kidd's, Grocer, Elm hill	Blickling, Wickmere, Hevingham, Marsham, &c.	F evg.	S	11
Pulham	15	Bailey	Cock, St. Stephen's	Newton, Tasburgh, Long Stratton, Wacton	Tu Th S	Tu Th S	2
Rackheath	5		Ludham Carrier				
Raynham	26		Thornham Carrier				
Reepham	14	Dennis	Crown and Scepter, St. Mic.	Swannington, Whitwell, Hackford, &c.	W S	W S	1
Reymerstone	12	White	White Lion, St. Benedict's	Barford, Carlton, Hardingham, Whindbergh, &c.	S mng.	S	1
Rockland	14	Fielding	Nag's Head, St. Stephen's	Wyndham, Attleborough, Ellingham, Caston, and Stow	F evng.	S	11
Saxlingham	7	Brock	Crown, St. Stephen's	Fritton, Stoke Holy Cross, &c.	S	S	2
		Dady	Star and Crown, Timberhill	Lakenham, Castor, Stoke, and Shottisham	W S	W S	1

Saxmundham	36		Halesworth Carrier				
Saxthorpe	15		Briston Carrier				
Scole	20		Diss Carrier				
Scottow	10		North Walsham Carrier				
Sherringham	20	Johnson	Lobster	St. Faith's, Aylsham, Cromer, &c.	W S	W S	12
Shipdham	20	Mendham	Woolpack, St. Giles'	Hingham, Watton, Swaffham, &c.	F. evng.	S	11
Shottisham	7	Crisp	Lion and Castle, Timberhill	Lakenham, Stoke, Castor, Framlingham	W S	W S	2
Skeyton	11	Bugden	King's Head, Magdalen-str.	Frettenham, Felmingham, &c.	S	S	2
Sloley	10		Coltishall Carrier				
Smallburgh	11	Law	Bull, Magdalen-street	Sprowston, Wroxham, Trunch, &c.	W S	W S	2
Southrepps	18	Jarvis	Ditto	Antingham, Felmingham, Mundesley, Northrepps	Tu F	W S	1
S. Walsham	10	Catton	White Lion, St. Mar. by Pal.	Blofield, Hemblington, &c.	S	S	2
		Ringer	Jolly Farmers, ditto	Ditto.	S	S	2
Southwold	30	Howlett	Star, Market-place	Wrentham, Benacre, Hempstead, Yarmouth	Tu	W	12
Spooner Row	13	Childerhouse	Woolpack, St. George's	Eaton, Hetherset, Wyndham, &c.	W S	W S	3
Stalham	16		Hingham Carrier				

Stanfield	22		Elmham Carrier				
Stowmarket	35	Hearn	White Hart, St. Peter's	Long Stratton, Scole, Thornham, Brockford, Needham, Claydon, Ipswich, from thence to London	Th	F	2
Stradbrook	28		Eye Carrier				
Stratton Strawl.	7		Hevingham Carrier				
Strumpshaw	9	Goffin	White Lion, St. Mar. by Pal.	Thorpe, Postwick, Brundle, and Lingwood	W mg.	W	12
Swaffham	28	Tiffen	White Lion, St. Benedict's	Dereham, Downham, Wisbech, &c.	Th ev.	F mg.	6
Swainthorpe	5		Long Stratton Carrier				
Swanton	10	Smith	King's Head, Magdalen-str.	Scottow, &c.	S	S	2
Swannington	8		Reepham Carrier				
Swanton Abbot	11	Spooner	Keys, Magdalen-street	Scottow, Westwick, Skeyton, Horstead, & Coltishall	S	S	2
Ditto Morley	13	Lock	Black Horse, St. Giles'		S	S	2
Swardeston	5		Buckenham Carrier				
Suffieldthorpe	13		Southrepps Carrier				
Taccolnestone	10	Nicholas	Yarmouth Bridge, R. Ln. lane	Swardeston, Mulbarton, Braconash, Ashwelthorpe,	S	S	4

				&c.			
Tasburgh	8	Hardy	Crown, St. Stephen's	Newton, &c.	S	S	2
Themilthorpe	14		Foulsham Carrier				
Thetford	30		London Wagons				
Thornham	40	Pointer	Wool-pack, St. Giles'	Drayton, Attlebridge, Sparham, Bawdeswell, Foxley, Fakenham, Docking, &c.	Tu mg.	Tu	2
Trunch	16		Southrepps Carrier				
Tullington	14		Skeyton Carrier				
Walsingham	27		Fakenham carrier				
Watton	21	Clarke	Currier's Arms, St. Giles'	Barford, Hingham, Swaffham, &c.	Tu F	W S	12
Watton	21	Sayer	Lobster	Wyndham, Hingham, Swaffham, Brandon	Tu F	W S	12
Wells	31	Lord	Woolpack, St. Giles'	Bawdeswell, Foxley, Snoring, Lenwade Bridge	Tu evg.	W	2
		Berrisfield	Pope's Head, Upper-market	Horsford, Caston Woodrow, Saxthorpe, Thornage, Field Dalling, &c.	Th	F evng.	6
		Allen	Wounded Heart, Up. mark.	Lenwade Bridge, Bawdeswell, Guist, Snoring, &c.	Tu Th	W F	4
Wyndham	9	Colman	Nag's Head, St. Stephen's	Eaton, Hetherset, Wicklewood, &c.	M W S	M W S	3

		Foulsham	Fortune of War, St. George's	Eaton, Cringleford, Hetherset, &c.	W S	W S	3
		Carter	Recruiting Sergt. St. Mary's	Eaton, Hetherset, &c.	S	S	4
		Rix	Cock, St. Stephen's	Ditto	M W S	M W S	3
Wisbech	54		Lynn Waggons				
Woodbridge	46		Ipswich Carrier				
Woolpit	40		Stowmarket Carrier				
Woolterton	14		Erpingham Carrier				
Worstead	12	Adams	White Horse, Magdalen-str.	Sprowston, Wroxham, Tunstead, &c.	S	S	3
Wrenningham	8		Buckenham Carrier				
York		Balls	Star, Market-place	Mansfield, Sheffield, Manchester, Birmingham, Nottingham, and the Principal Towns in Yorkshire	Tu F	Tu F	3
Yarmouth	22		Acle Carrier				
Yaxham	15		Dereham Carrier				

FOOTNOTES

[0] There is no map in the copy at Norwich, although this heading implies there may have originally been a map of some sort.—DP.

[42] In the Norwich Millennium Library copy someone has written in a very neat hand at the bottom of page 42: "Hooke Peter, Surry St."—DP.

[49] There appear to have never been pages 47 and 48. From the way the directory is bound at Norwich the printer probably left a gap in the pagination to cope with any last minute additions.—DP.

CPSIA information can be obtained
at www.ICGtesting.com
Printed in the USA
LVHW031742010323
740520LV00003B/869